Gaining Decisions for Christ

Gaining
Decisions
for
Christ

A HOW-TO MANUAL

Louis R. Torres

REVIEW AND HERALD® PUBLISHING ASSOCIATION
HAGERSTOWN, MD 21740

The author assumes full responsibility for the accuracy of
all facts and quotations as cited in this book.

This book was
Edited by Jeannette Johnson
Copyedited by Lori Halvorsen and James Cavil
Cover and interior design by Bill Kirstein
Electronic makeup by Shirley M. Bolivar
Typeset: 12/14 Bembo

PRINTED IN U.S.A.

05   04   03   02   01   5   4   3   2   1

R&H Cataloging Service
Torres, Louis R
      Gaining decisions for Christ: a how-to manual

      1. Evangelistic work. 2. Witness bearing (Christianity)   I. Title

                              253

ISBN 0-8280-1633-X

Dedication

Of all the people who have impacted my life, none have had a greater influence than four women.

My mother, Elsa,
passed away a year ago. She was handicapped because of a lack of formal education, as well as her physical ailments. But one handicap she did not have: She knew how to talk with God. Her prayer life sustained her while she raised six boys in the heart of the ghettos.

My wife, Carol,
has been with me through thick and thin during the past 30 years. Her indomitable spirit has inspired me to go on when others felt I had no future. She is great soul winner in her own right. Much credit that has been bestowed on me really should have gone to her.

My daughter, Talitha,
—Daddy's girl—has grown up to become a mother of four. Her strong belief in me and her constant encouragement have enabled me to keep moving forward and upward.

My dear mother-in-law, Beatrice Reinke, (better known as Grandma), is a deeply spiritual woman with a burden for souls. She has inspired me with her love and tenacity for the holy Word.

To these four queens, I dedicate this book.

Contents

Chapter 1

Soul Winning Brings Reciprocal Blessings

My brother Gene and I left home with our fishing gear, headed to the Far Rockaway Bridge. Once at our destination, we unpacked our lures and opened up the bait bag. As a Brooklyn ghetto boy, I didn't know much about fishing. However, the presence of my big brother gave me confidence that I'd get the best course on the art. With a baited hook and sinker, I followed his example and cast my line into the water. After a few moments I squealed in excitement and began to reel in what I was sure to be the biggest fish ever! Seaweed—that's all it was. I re-cast and reeled in again, only to find that this time the bait was missing. While I was casting for what seemed to be the umpteenth time, it started to rain. We hid under an umbrella we had brought "just in case," and waited for the rain to subside. As the rain increased, my brother decided to pull in his line and let it dangle out of the water.

Once the rain stopped, Gene reeled in his line to re-cast. As he looked down the side of the bridge to spot how far down his line was, he burst into excited laughter. Unbeknown to him, a large fish had become snagged underneath on the hook. He had caught a fish by default.

Just as my brother, many a sincere Christian worker ventures out to fish for people with just as little know-how as Gene and I possessed of fishing. No doubt some fish can be caught by default, but how much better if before going fishing one can be prepared with experiential skills, affording a home return filled with the rejoicing of "bringing in the sheaves."

For many, fishing is an exciting pastime, but the excitement that comes from leading a soul to Christ far surpasses any other thrill. It is the most rewarding experience that a Christian can have. The joy of watching a person accept Jesus can be compared to the happiness of a mother after she travails in birth and brings a new child into the world. It is said of Jesus, "He shall see of the travail of his soul, and shall be satisfied" (Isa. 53:11). Christ was willing to endure hardship in order to "seek . . . that which was lost" (Luke 19:10). Seeing souls won gave Him the highest joy. The apostle Paul wrote, "Looking unto Jesus the author and finisher of our faith; who for the joy that was set before him endured the cross, despising the shame, and is set down at the right hand of the throne of God" (Heb. 12:2). "He values this recompense so highly that He forgets the anguish it has cost Him to redeem fallen man." [1] Jesus had, and still has, a consuming burden for souls. It was this compelling concern for the lost sinner that caused the Son of God to leave heaven. All those in the celestial courts also share His joy. "Likewise, I say unto you," Jesus said, "there is joy in the presence of the angels of God over one sinner that repenteth" (Luke 15:10).

It is this same burden and resulting joy that is born into the heart of one who receives Christ as their personal Saviour. Once the desire for souls is implanted in the heart, it erupts into spontaneous action, stirring the believer to do the same as his Master. "The one work more precious than any other is the work of soul-saving. The same intensity of desire for the saving of souls that marked the life of the

Saviour marks the life of His true followers. The Christian has no desire to live for self. He delights to consecrate all he has and is to the Master's service. He is moved with an inexpressible desire to win souls to Christ. Those who have nothing of this desire might better be concerned for their own salvation. Let them pray for the spirit of service."[2]

When one labors for the salvation of others, eternal blessings are yielded not only to the recipient of the labor but also to the laborers themselves. The prophet Daniel wrote: "And they that be wise shall shine as the brightness of the firmament; and they that turn many to righteousness as the stars for ever and ever" (Dan. 12:3). Jesus stated: "And he that reapeth receiveth wages, and gathereth fruit unto life eternal: that both he that soweth and he that reapeth may rejoice together" (John 4:36). "There are rich blessings in store for those who surrender fully to the call of God. As such workers endeavor to win souls to Jesus, they will find that many who never could have been reached in any other way are ready to respond to intelligent personal effort."[3]

King David understood the direct correlation between his spiritual life and his effectiveness in soul winning. He prayed, "Purge me with hyssop, and I shall be clean: wash me, and I shall be whiter than snow. Make me to hear joy and gladness; that the bones which thou hast broken may rejoice. Hide thy face from my sins, and blot out all mine iniquities. Create in me a clean heart, O God; and renew a right spirit within me. Cast me not away from thy presence; and take not thy holy spirit from me" (Ps. 51:7-11). Usually people stop here when reading this passage as a scripture reading in church. But notice the next two verses. David continues, "Restore unto me the joy of thy salvation; and uphold me with thy free spirit. *Then will I teach transgressors thy ways; and sinners shall be converted unto thee"* (verses 12, 13). In other words, receiving an answer to his prayer enables him to win souls. This is why he concludes with "then will I teach transgressors." This is the natural outcome of true prayer. The benefits of soul winning are reciprocal in nature—as you receive truth you give to others, and as you give, you will receive blessings in return.

This human cooperation with divinity for the salvation of souls is one of God's chosen means for re-creating in His children the character of Christ. There is no doubt that *"God could have reached His object in saving sinners without our aid; but in order for us to develop a character like Christ's, we must share in His work. In order to enter into His joy—the joy of seeing souls redeemed by His sacrifice—we must participate in His labors for their redemption."*[4] This is an imperative. We are told, "When the character of Christ shall be perfectly reproduced in His people, then He will come to claim them as His own."[5] A Christlike character is the prerequisite for heaven, and it is what Christ is waiting for His followers on earth to develop before He can return. If this is true, then how essential is it to our character to be involved in the work of soul saving? Is it possible to develop a likeness to Christ without participating in this work? The answer is obvious. Being involved in this labor provides an essential element for spiritual growth that leads to the development of a Christlike character. It is like nutrition—each of the vitamins is essential to good health. Vitamins E, C, and D provide nutrition that vitamin B cannot provide, but that does not make vitamin B nonessential. Just as each vitamin must be present for the body to obtain optimal health, so also the different elements of Christianity—including active witnessing—must be present for the Christian to reach spiritual health.

"Those who are most actively employed in doing with interested fidelity their work to win souls to Jesus Christ are the best developed in spirituality and devotion. Their very active working formed the means of their spirituality."[6] Hence, "the only way to grow in grace is to be disinterestedly doing the very work which Christ has enjoined upon us—to engage, to the extent of our ability, in helping and blessing those who need the help we can give them. Strength comes by exercise; activity is the very condition of life. Those who endeavor to maintain a Christian life by passively accepting the blessings that come through the means of grace, and do nothing for Christ, are simply trying to live by eating without working. And in the spiritual world, as in the natural, this always results in degeneration and decay. A man who would refuse to exercise his limbs would soon lose all power to use them. Thus the Christian who will not exercise his God-given powers not only fails to grow up into Christ, but he loses the strength that he already had."[7] "One of the divine plans for growth is impartation. The Christian is to gain strength by strengthening others. 'He that watereth shall be watered also himself.' This is not merely a promise; it is a divine law, a law by which God designs that the streams of benevolence, like the waters of the great deep, shall be kept in constant circulation, continually flowing back to their source. In the fulfilling of this law is the secret of spiritual growth."[8] To sum it up, "we become overcomers by helping others to overcome, by the blood of the Lamb and the word of our testimony."[9] The promise states: "They that sow in tears shall reap in joy. He that goeth forth and weepeth, bearing precious seed, shall doubtless come again with rejoicing, bringing his sheaves with him" (Psalm 126:5, 6).

---

[1] *The Seventh-day Adventist Bible Commentary,* Ellen G. White Comments, vol. 5, p. 1146.

[2] Ellen G. White, in *Australasian Union Conference Record,* Aug. 15, 1902.

[3] ———, *The Acts of the Apostles,* p. 158.

[4] ———, *The Desire of Ages,* p. 142. (Italics supplied.)

[5] ———, *Christ's Object Lessons,* p. 69.

[6] ———, *Evangelism,* p. 356.

[7] ———, *Steps to Christ,* pp. 80, 81.

[8] ———, in *Signs of the Times,* June 12, 1901.

[9] ———, Ellen G. White letter 236, 1908.

Chapter 2

Working for Souls Is Challenging

Leading a soul to Christ is not exactly the simplest task that can be undertaken. If it were, then every church member would be filled with joy and the work of God would have probably already been finished. But because of the demands of time, talent, and energy, a large percentage of believers fail to get involved. There are those who have attempted to reach others out of a mere sense of duty, but they have been left disappointed by unsuccessful experiences. Too often those who have "tried their hand" at soul winning and have tasted failure conclude that this occupation should be left only to the trained, educated pastor or evangelist. But "the work of saving souls is not confined to the delegated ministers. To every man God has given his work. Every soul that has been enlightened has a work to do, a mission to perform. Each one is to trade diligently with the talents entrusted to his care. Converted himself, the Christian is to present to others the truth as it is in Christ Jesus, and win souls to Jesus."[1]

"The Saviour's commission to the disciples included all the believers. It includes all believers in Christ to the end of time. It is a *fatal mistake* to suppose that the work of saving souls depends alone on the ordained minister. All to whom the heavenly inspiration has come are put in trust with the gospel. All who receive the life of Christ are or-

dained to work for the salvation of their fellow men. For this work the church was established, and all who take upon themselves its sacred vows are thereby pledged to be coworkers with Christ."[2] "Every true disciple is born into the kingdom of God as a missionary. He who drinks of the living water becomes a fountain of life. The receiver becomes a giver. The grace of Christ in the soul is like a spring in the desert, welling up to refresh all, and making those who are ready to perish eager to drink of the water of life."[3] "Every church member should feel it his special duty to labor for those living in his neighborhood. Study how you can best help those who take no interest in religious things. As you visit your friends and neighbors show an interest in their spiritual as well as in their temporal welfare. Present Christ as a sin-pardoning Saviour. . . . Let church members educate themselves to do this work. This is just as essential as to save the benighted souls in foreign countries."[4] "All are to represent Christ in active, earnest effort to save perishing souls."[5]

Preaching in Apostolic Times Done by the Laity

In the early church the laity carried the primary responsibility of spreading the gospel beyond the borders of Jerusalem. Contrary to general assumption, the apostles did not do all of this work. The Scripture verifies: "Therefore *they that were scattered abroad went everywhere preaching the word*" (Acts 8:4). The question we must answer is Who were these scattered ones who went everywhere preaching? In Acts we are told, "And Saul was consenting unto his [Stephen's] death. And at that time there was a great persecution against the church which was in Jerusalem; and *they were all scattered abroad throughout the regions of Judea and Samaria, except the apostles*" (verse 1). The apostle Paul is the "Saul" mentioned here. Obviously, he was not yet involved in the propagation of the gospel. Since it states "except the apostles," we must conclude that the rank and file of the members did the preaching. In fact, the man named Philip mentioned later in this chapter, who met the Ethiopian and baptized him, was Philip the deacon, not Philip the apostle.

This lay preaching movement was in perfect harmony with the commission given by Christ. Jesus declared, "Go ye into all the world, and preach the gospel to every creature" (Mark 16:15). The believers in His day concluded that these marching orders pertained to all of them. Their understanding of the word "preach" was much different than the definition people conjure up today. The early believer's idea of preaching was not relegated merely to standing behind a podium and delivering a weekly message. Philip found the Ethiopian eunuch traveling in a chariot and that is where he "preached," or shared with him. It was in the streets of Jerusalem that Peter delivered the Pentecost message, and then he later shared the hope of salvation in the home of the centurion. Preaching was not as limited in its scope as some so narrowly think today. Jesus shared in the marketplace, in personal homes, in local synagogues, by village wells, on grassy hillsides, and by the seaside. This biblical preaching can be carried out today at the gas station, at the factory, in the classroom, by the fireside, and so on. In other words, anyone can share the good news of salvation in any place.

The word *preach,* when used in biblical context, can have a few different meanings. Its definitions include: "to talk," "a discourse," "to cry or proclaim," "to bring or tell good news," and "to announce thoroughly."[6] In fact, a quick perusal of Scripture reveals that the word *preach* is not even found in the three lists of spiritual gifts mentioned in the New Testament. One of these lists states: "For to one is given by the Spirit the word of wisdom; to another the word of knowledge by the same Spirit; to another faith by the same Spirit; to another the gifts of healing by the same Spirit; to another the working of miracles; to another prophecy; to another discerning of spirits; to another divers kinds of tongues; to another the interpretation of tongues" (1 Corinthians 12:8-10). Romans 12:6-8 says, "Having then gifts differing according to the grace that is given to us, whether prophecy, let us prophesy according to the proportion of faith; or ministry, let us wait on our ministering: or he that teacheth, on teaching; or he that exhorteth, on exhortation; he that giveth, let him do it with simplicity; he that ruleth, with diligence; he that showeth mercy, with cheerfulness." The third list tells us, "And he gave some, apostles; and some, prophets; and some, evangelists; and some, pastors and teachers" (Ephesians 4:11).

Why is the word *preach* not given here? Because all the believers are to be endowed with this gift, with the zeal to share. This ability to speak for God is received as soon as a love for Jesus is born in the heart. The woman who met Jesus at the well ran to spread the good news in her village. The liberated demoniac went home and told his friends and family the "great things" God had done for him (Mark 5:19). The blind man, after receiving his sight, preached eloquently to church leaders concerning Jesus. John the revelator states, "And the Spirit and the bride say, Come. And let him that heareth *say, Come.* And let him that is athirst come. And whosoever will, let him take the water of life freely" (Revelation 22:17). Notice that the one who responds to what he hears is not only to come, but also to *say,* "Come." It is the privilege of every believer to participate in giving the invitation.

Not all will preach in the same way, but all are commissioned to share the love of Jesus. There may be some who are given the special gift of evangelism. They can deliver the message more effectively through that avenue. Others will be given other talents. The Scripture says, "For to one is given by the Spirit the word of wisdom; to another the word of knowledge by the same Spirit; to another faith by the same Spirit; to another the gifts of healing by the same Spirit; to another the working of miracles; to another prophecy; to another discerning of spirits; to another divers kinds of tongues; to another the interpretation of tongues" (1 Corinthians 12:8-10). But irrespective of the gift given, they each are channels through which preaching can be accomplished. A teacher can "preach" to those whom the mechanic may never reach, but the mechanic will associate with people a pastor might never meet. We are admonished to "invite your neighbors to your home, and read with them from the precious Bible and from books that explain its truths. Invite them to unite with you in song and prayer. In these little gatherings, Christ Himself will be present, as He has promised, and hearts will be touched by His grace."[7]

One day while I was visiting a church I happened to glance at a sign the pastor had placed on the bulletin board. It read, "Few come to church to get involved; few stay if they don't." Therefore, I believe that extending the invitation to others and sharing the Word to win others to Christ is something that all of us can, and should, do. This is possible because "every true disciple is born into the kingdom of God as a missionary. He who drinks of the living water becomes a fountain of life. The receiver becomes a giver.

The grace of Christ in the soul is like a spring in the desert, welling up to refresh all, and making those who are ready to perish eager to drink of the water of life."[8] For "all who receive the gospel message into the heart will long to proclaim it. The heaven-born love of Christ must find expression."[9]

"Thus Christ gave His disciples their commission. He made full provision for the prosecution of the work, and took upon Himself the responsibility for its success. So long as they obeyed His word, and worked in connection with Him, they could not fail. Go to all nations, He bade them. Go to the farthest part of the habitable globe, but know that My presence will be there. Labor in faith and confidence, for the time will never come when I will forsake you."[10] What a precious promise this is to all who are willing to yoke up with Christ!

[1] Ellen G. White, in *Review and Herald*, Dec. 12, 1893.
[2] ———, *The Desire of Ages*, p. 822. (Italics supplied.)
[3] ———, *Christian Service*, p. 9.
[4] ———, *Welfare Ministry*, p. 190.
[5] ———, *Testimonies to Ministers and Gospel Workers*, p. 163.
[6] *Strong's Exhaustive Concordance.*
[7] White, *Christian Service*, p. 112.
[8] ———, *The Desire of Ages*, p. 195.
[9] ———, *Christ's Object Lessons*, p. 125.
[10] ———, *The Desire of Ages*, p. 822.

Chapter 3

A Science to Soul Winning

There is a science to soul winning. As essential as it is to get involved in sharing Christ, it is equally important to consider this point. Each discipline of study has its rules and laws that contribute to its successful employment, and so it is with soul winning. "Of all sciences, the highest and the most essential is the science of soul saving. It embraces very much. In your position of trust you need to learn more concerning this science; for you need to exert a molding influence over every one with whom you have anything to do. But in order to do justice to this work, you must first learn of Christ."[1] In order to be a participant in this work, we must become acquainted with the basic do's of this science. And the opposite is just as true. Learning what not to do can help us avoid many common mistakes made by others.

Leading Others to Make Decisions

Leading a person to make a decision in favor of the gospel involves several steps. One of the most important of these considerations is the person's personal experience. To know where the individual is in their experience is paramount. People are in different stages and cycles of life. They are not all marching to the same drumbeat. All have different needs. Because of this, we must "become acquainted with the people in their homes. Test the spiritual pulse."[2]

Hence, it is essential that the one who is seeking to lead others to Christ also be able to discern where the person is experientially. This means that an effort must be made to ascertain where the candidate is in their spiritual walk. To accomplish this, one must come close to the people. We are admonished to visit every family and learn the status of their spiritual condition. "Wherever a church is established, all the members should engage actively in a missionary work. They should visit every family in the neighborhood and know their spiritual condition. If professed Christians had engaged in this work from the time when their names were first placed on the church books, there would not now be such widespread unbelief, such depths of iniquity, such unparalleled wickedness, as is seen in the world at the present time. If every church member had sought to enlighten others, thousands upon thousands would today stand with God's commandment-keeping people."[3] As we become acquainted with a person's social and spiritual condition, it places us in a better position to help them.

---

[1] Ellen G. White, *The Ellen G. White 1888 Materials,* vol. 4, p. 1788.
[2] ———, *Evangelism,* p. 142.
[3] ———, *Welfare Ministry,* pp. 71, 72.

Chapter 4

Categorizing Your Candidates

Once we determine the level of a person's spiritual condition, we should then categorize them. Doing this does not arbitrarily lock everyone into these categories, or pigeonhole them. People are in a constant state of flux. However, this categorizing serves to aid the soul winner in becoming more directed in his/her efforts. It will also enable the worker in facilitating an appropriate plan and the right approach to take.

For our purpose in this book, we will divide the potential candidates into one of three categories. There is usually some overlapping. However, while there may be overlap in some cases, most people fall rather cleanly into one of the basic categories:

1. Sow
2. Cultivate
3. Harvest

The ones in the *sow* category are those who need to have the seed of God's Word planted in their minds—the people who have never heard. It is amazing that although we live in such a religion-saturated society, there are still those who have never been taught anything about the Bible. I have met many individuals who grew up in religiously deprived homes. Their knowledge of God is often distorted, or else they are completely ignorant of His existence.

23

The second group takes in those who need *cultivation* and nurturing. These are people who have heard the gospel but need more information and more spiritual growth. They may already be members of a church or religious society, or perhaps they are seeking God independently. Nevertheless, they need to grow in grace in order to bring them to the next level. This brings us to the third category.

This group is comprised of those who need to be *harvested*. These are individuals sufficiently informed, but who have not made a decision to commit themselves fully to Christ. They have not been led to the step of commitment, or have not understood how to practice and internalize the truths they understand.

We will be addressing these three categories in succeeding chapters. I will also try to give insights on how to categorize your contacts, and what to do with them afterward. But let me hasten to warn—do not seek to depend on the mechanics or the techniques. While guidelines are helpful, they cannot take the place of your own need to develop a perceptive spirit. Discernment will go a long way in helping you accurately evaluate people as you work with them.

The importance of ascertaining a person's experiential level becomes quite evident through the following examples. Let's suppose you come across an atheist. Urging him to make a commitment to Christ as his Saviour when he does not even believe in the existence of God is futile! The same is true with those individuals who need sowing. Trying to cultivate commitment where no seed has been planted will most certainly result in wasted efforts. And the converse is also true. Spending time with someone who has already heard and believes truth, and using that time solely in actions of sowing seed, will result in frustration to you, and perhaps in insult to the candidate. It is equivalent to belaboring the most basic math concepts with one who has already mastered algebra.

This need to develop a personal sense of discernment cannot be overstressed. This sensitivity to others comes as a result of maintaining a growing personal relationship with the Lord. Study time, experience, and much prayer are the main contributing factors to developing this ability. The Lord has promised that talents used for His glory will bring multiplied talents. One must become attuned to the workings of God's Spirit on human hearts. Techniques and methodology have their place, but they cannot substitute this personal encounter with Christ. Having personally felt and understood the moving of God in your own life endows you with a greater ability to decipher. This is something that each one of us must develop. Though there are many methods and tools available for our work with souls, one cannot depend on a proxy-oriented approach. Nothing can take the place of the gift of tender discrimination, and a heart filled with the warmth of Jesus. Remember—it is not the tool that does the work, but rather the person who must develop the expertise to work the tool.

Application of the Categories

Let us examine how to put this into practical application. One day you are talking with a person, and after brief discussion you discern that they are ripe for decision. If they are at an experience level where they can be encouraged to make the decision, then the necessary methods for reaping should be used. If, however, this person has never been exposed to Christ's truth, then adequate sowing techniques should be employed. If a person demonstrates spiritual awareness, yet is not at a point of complete surrender to the Lord, then appropriate programs or processes to induce greater growth should be implemented.

On page 27 is a chart outlining precisely what we are talking about. Notice the programs under *sowing*. The church, for the purpose of planting seeds, has developed most of its programs under this category. The seed, of course, represents the Word of God (see Luke 8:11). Each seed-sowing program is designed to reach people according to their felt needs. Many individuals would never voluntarily cast their shadow on the steps of a church. But they might comfortably attend a health seminar held by the church in a neutral setting. Consequently, these programs afford opportunities to approach candidates in a nonthreatening environment so seeds can be planted. Once the seed has been sown by means of these contact-point programs, it needs to be cultivated. That's the next segment in our chart.

Notice that the number of *cultivating* programs is fewer than those listed in the *sowing* category. And so it is with the *harvest*. The process of soul winning generally funnels itself down to one-on-one contact. Once the sequence begins, the process must be encouraged to continue its natural course. It is the Word of God, once planted in the soul and cultivated, that finally bears the fruit of conversion. The Word *must* become flesh. Since this is the ultimate goal, the candidate must at some point be led into the study of the Word itself. The focus must be transferred from the healing of felt needs to their need of spiritual renewal and the importance of accepting salvation. This can be facilitated through those programs intended for cultivation.

Sometimes a *sowing* program, such as the Stop

Smoking Plan, can be used as a cultivator. For instance, usually there are smokers among the audiences of my evangelistic meetings. Recognizing this, I will offer a separate program during the second week to help them overcome their habit. They don't understand my reasons for offering the additional program, but I know I am providing them help that will enable them to be free from the shackle of smoking; at the same time this gives me the opportunity to help them grow in grace. They need to overcome the sinful habit so they will be free to make a total commitment when I call for decisions. During the sessions I tie in the scriptural reasons for quitting. Once they have gained victory through the power of Christ, it is much easier for them to become victorious in other difficult areas. And so a program normally used for sowing is turned into a means of cultivation.

SOWING	CULTIVATING	HARVESTING
Stop-smoking program		
Cooking classes		
Weight-control program	Bible studies	
Stress classes	Revelation seminars	Evangelistic Mtg.
Literature	Daniel seminars	One-on-one
Radio/TV programs	Radio/TV	
Disaster relief	Literature	
Language schools		
Friendship		

In the *harvest* phase there are no effective means of reaping outside of Bible study or evangelistic meetings. These ultimately progress into the "one-on-one" approach. Again, always remember that you must determine where people are. Once you have ascertained their interest level, use the proper methods needed to further accomplish your God-given task of soul winning.

The Need to Watch

Our ultimate goal is always to lead a person to the point of decision. However, to do this effectively, one must learn to watch and observe. But if you have already categorically placed your candidate according to their readiness, why continue to watch so closely? Because people can change in a moment. Consider the following scenario.

A particular man is an atheist. Everything is going all right for him. He is quite well off financially, has a nice home and a good position at work. But one day he comes home and finds a brief Dear John note on the kitchen counter. Reading it, he discovers that his wife has abandoned him. What happens to him next? The sudden trauma may awaken him to the reality that something in his life is missing. He starts to think that perhaps he *does* need God, that maybe there is a stronger Power—and so he begins his search for something greater on which to lean.

Here is a second example. *I was speaking in a church for Wednesday night prayer meeting when a derelict was brought in from the street. An early-arriving member waiting for the church to open had seen the homeless man stumble and fall. Jumping out of his car, he picked him up from the gutter. While he was debating what to do next, the church doors opened. Moved with compassion, he determined to help the stranger. But first he needed to attend prayer meeting and would have to take him along, so he brought his charge into the church service. That night, after my presentation, I made an appeal asking those who desired to give their lives to Christ to stand up. The derelict was the first to respond, and that was the last time he drank alcohol. Though he'd previously been hospitalized and detoxified 10 different times, he had always returned to his old habit. But his first encounter with Christ made a lifetime difference.*

A similar situation occurred at another prayer meeting.

After the message a visitor approached me and requested a few minutes of my time. Telling me that this was his first visit to the church in 50 years, he revealed that two weeks earlier his wife had passed away. Her death was so traumatic for him that he had finally realized his spiritual void and decided to seek for God.

There is no question that people can change. And the change can occur overnight—almost instantaneously! Consequently, we must learn to be observant. Watch! Be watching all the time. We are told, "You should watch and see if there is an interest in this one or that." * This is the essence of evangelism! You may be asking, "What do you specifically watch for?" The answer—you must learn to discern the moving of God's Spirit! This moving is defined in one word—*conviction*. The one important factor—the most essential element to watch for—is the evidence of conviction.

---

* Ellen G. White, *Evangelism,* p. 185.

Chapter 5

Conviction:
The Most
Essential Element

The most significant element necessary for a person to make a true spiritual decision is the element of conviction. Without divine conviction, no one can be brought to make a genuine commitment to God. Conviction is the means by which sinners are made aware of their true condition. It is the unseen compelling force that stirs the heart into action. It arouses the emotions and tugs at the soul. John 16:8 demonstrates the relevancy of conviction. "And when he is come, he will reprove [convict] the world of sin, and of righteousness, and of judgment." God's Spirit is the power that convicts us of sin, righteousness, and judgment. That is, He brings to our attention what is wrong in us—(sin), what is right in us through Him (righteousness), and our need to make a decision between the two (judgment).

Conviction is the voice of God speaking to the conscience. Therefore, it is imperative that each worker for souls becomes personally acquainted with it. We should gain by experience a knowledge of the prompting of the Holy Spirit. Ask yourself, "Have I personally been convicted? How did I feel?" And when experiencing conviction, "How did I respond?" Then, if you have experienced His promptings, it will aid you in detecting the Spirit's influence in the lives of others. This personal knowledge will also enable you to help others recognize it in their own hearts and thus be encouraged to respond appropriately. Once we are equipped with this sensitivity and have the ability to observe it in others, we can know what course of action should be followed to effectively facilitate maturation into a committed decision. If you are not cognizant of the presence of conviction, you may find yourself "pulling in the line when there is nothing hooked on the other end." You may be drawing in seaweed and thinking you have a big fish on the line. Possessing this personal awareness of conviction and the indicators of its presence is rudimentary. Without it, you simply won't know when to call for a decision. Anyone who has become a Christian has felt or experienced conviction at one time or another. If you, the reader, have experienced this prompting in your own life, then you are in a better position to recognize it in those to whom you are witnessing. And once you have noticed it in your own life, you can empathetically minister to others.

The Phenomenon of Conviction

How do we observe the phenomenon of conviction? One night Jesus had a visitor. "There was a man of the Pharisees, named Nicodemus, a ruler of the Jews: The same came to Jesus by night, and said unto him, Rabbi, we know that thou art a teacher come from God: for no man can do these miracles that thou doest, except God be with him. Jesus answered and said unto him, Verily, verily, I say unto thee, Except a man be born again, he cannot see the kingdom of God. Nicodemus saith unto him, How can a man be born when he is old? can he enter the second time into his mother's womb, and be born? Jesus answered, Verily, verily, I say unto thee, Except a man be born of water and of the Spirit, he cannot enter into the kingdom of God" (John 3:1-5).

Nicodemus did not understand. So Jesus continued, "That which is born of the flesh is flesh; and that which is born of the Spirit is spirit. Marvel not that I said unto thee, Ye must be born again. The wind bloweth where it listeth, and thou hearest the sound thereof, but canst not tell whence it cometh, and whither it goeth: so is every one that is born of the Spirit" (verses 6-8). Here the Lord gives us an insight into the workings of the Holy Ghost. "Like the wind, which is invisible, yet the effects of which are plainly seen and felt, is the Spirit of God in its work upon the human heart. That regenerating power, which no human eye can see, begets a new life in the soul; it creates a new being in the image of God. While the work of the Spirit is silent and imperceptible, its effects are manifest."[1] It is obvious that no one can see the wind. However, its presence and movements can be observed by the sound, or by its effect on objects. So it is with the effect of the Holy Spirit working in humans. While it is true that no one can see the Spirit working on the human heart, His presence can be observed by the outward manifestations of the recipient. If a tree is moving, then we know that the wind is blowing. If the tree is still, then the opposite is true—no wind is present. The wind, then, represents the Spirit and the tree, a person under the Spirit's influence. In Psalm 1:3 we read, "And he shall be like a *tree* planted by the rivers of water, that bringeth forth his fruit in his season; his leaf also shall not wither; and whatsoever he doeth shall prosper." From these statements in Scripture we can conclude that the workings of the Holy Spirit are definitely observable.

"Christ is the source of every right impulse. He is the only one that can implant in the heart enmity against sin. Every desire for truth and purity, every conviction of our own sinfulness, is an evidence that His Spirit is moving upon our hearts."[2] Therefore, "every fresh display of the conviction of the grace of God upon the souls of unbelievers is divine."[3] If it is a display, then it is noticeable—we should be able to see it. Notice this statement: "Though we cannot see the Spirit of God, we know that men who have been dead in trespasses and sins become convicted and converted under its operations. The thoughtless and wayward become serious. The hardened repent of their sins, and the faithless believe. The gambler, the drunkard, the licentious, become steady, sober, and pure. The rebellious and obstinate become meek and Christlike. When we see these changes in the character, we may be assured that the converting power of God has transformed the entire man. We saw not the Holy Spirit, but we saw the evidence of its work on the changed character of those who were hardened and obdurate sinners. As the wind moves in its force upon the lofty trees and brings them down, so the Holy Spirit can work upon human hearts, and no finite man can circumscribe the work of God."[4]

As I have observed individuals giving Bible studies, I have noticed that their tendency is to focus on disseminating information. This takes place because they have not been trained to watch for the moving of God's Spirit. Somehow they suppose that the entire substance of their task is to get through the 24 lessons, and so they inadvertently concentrate on that alone. Consequently, they expect that upon completion of the course the student will immediately ask, "Where is the baptistry?" But this is not the normal outcome. Most of the time the student may express gratitude for time spent, but will make no commitment to follow the teachings learned. The result is that the one giving the studies is left disappointed, or becomes discouraged. This often leads them to wonder if they are following their calling after all. Or they may erroneously decide that the student is simply rejecting truth. Obviously then, being information-oriented instead of being Spirit-directed can, and usually does, result in frustrated efforts.

"The preaching of the word will be of no avail without the continual presence and aid of the Holy Spirit. This is the only effectual teacher of divine truth. Only when the truth is accompanied to the heart by the Spirit will it quicken the conscience or transform the life. One might be able to present the letter of the word of God, he might be familiar with all its commands and promises; but unless the Holy Spirit sets home the truth, no souls will fall on the Rock and be broken. No amount of education, no advantages, however great, can make one a channel of light without the cooperation of the Spirit of God. The sowing of the gospel seed will not be a success unless the seed is quickened into life by the dew of heaven."[5]

This principle corresponds to the laws of nature. In many deserts seeds lie dormant until a rain shower drops its life-giving moisture. It isn't long before the desert is covered with gorgeous blossoms. The same is true with farming. It takes moisture to activate the seeds into growth that will eventually bear fruit for the harvest.

Therefore, to have greater success in soul winning we must learn to cooperate with, and watch for, the moving of the Spirit as His influence is demonstrated by the corresponding response of the hearer. It is said of Christ, *"Jesus watched with deep earnestness the changing countenances of His hearers. The faces that expressed interest and pleasure, gave Him great satisfaction. As the arrows of truth pierced to the soul, breaking through the barriers of selfishness, and working contrition, and finally gratitude, the Saviour was made glad."*[6] *"He spoke di-*

rectly to every mind and appealed to every heart. He watched the faces of His hearers, marked the lighting up of the countenance, the quick, responsive glance, which told that truth had reached the soul; and there vibrated in His heart the answering chord of sympathetic joy." [7]

This lesson was one I had to learn early in my ministry. At first I was focused predominately on making sure that I delivered the right information. Since my nose was in my notes, my eyes could not observe my audience. While it is true that accurate perception is a skill honed through practice and experience, the sooner that presenters of biblical truths learn to watch their listeners, the more quickly their effectiveness will develop. So then, as you sit and give a Bible study or preach a message, you must watch and observe the body language and actions of whomever you are trying to communicate with. These visible signs are observable indicators that conviction is present. This insight will give greater confidence to you, the worker. For when you are aware that the Spirit is actively working in the candidate, it brings excitement and hope. This certainty will also provide greater conviction on your part as the speaker, serving in turn as a strong incentive to make appeals.

Visible Indicators of Conviction

Let us now consider some concrete evidences of the outworking of conviction. Usually when people come under the influence of the Holy Spirit, they tend to demonstrate His presence through both negative and positive responses. Notice this chart of typical responses.

Positive Indicators	*Negative Indicators*
1. Joy	1. Sorrow
2. Sharing/Telling Others	2. Rejection

3. Personal Application
4. Tears
5. Can't Stay Away
6. Lighting Up of Face
7. Becoming Friendly
8. Questions
9. Studying
10. Positive
    Attitude
    Changes
11. Lifestyle Changes
12. Restitution
13. Peace
14. Praying About It

3. Argument
4. Tears
5. Avoidance
6. Anger
7. Resistance
8. Objections
9. Refusal to Study
10. Negative
    Attitude
    Changes
11. Rebellion
12. Denial
13. Restlessness
14. Irritability

Notice all the different ways that people respond to conviction. Most of the time people assume that there are only positive responses to the Spirit. But while it is true that the outcome may be positive, there is no doubt that negative reactions are often exhibited as well. As an observer I must watch to see if the "tree" is moving in the wind. Are there positive or negative responses? What are the evidences of the Holy Spirit's presence? You must ask yourself, Can I see any physical exhibitions? What emotional demonstrations are taking place? Is there squirming, nervousness, anger, or fear? Are new teachings being put into action in the candidate's life? Is it being internalized and practiced? Is there silence or crying, avoiding or bargaining? Are they making an attempt to rationalize? Is joy or sorrow being experienced? Are they sharing what they've learned with others? Do they demonstrate a new peace, or make any effort to stop sinning?

An accurate recognition of these different responses is

as essential as knowing the difference between when a fish is biting your bait or the water's current is dragging the line. The following statements reinforce this concept. *"The Spirit of God is manifested in different ways upon different men. One under the movings of this power will tremble before the Word of God. His convictions will be so deep that a hurricane and tumult of feeling seem to rage in his heart, and his whole being is prostrate under the convicting power of the truth. When the Lord speaks forgiveness to the repenting soul, he is full of ardor, full of love to God, full of earnestness and energy, and the life-giving spirit which he has received cannot be repressed."*[8] Here is another statement demonstrating the opposite. *"All are not constituted alike. Conversions are not all alike. Jesus impresses the heart, and the sinner is born again to new life. Often souls have been drawn to Christ when there was no violent conviction, no soul rending, no remorseful terrors. They looked upon an uplifted Saviour; they lived. They saw the soul's need; they saw the Saviour's sufficiency and His claims; they heard His voice saying, 'Follow Me,' and they rose up and followed Him. This conversion was genuine, and the religious life was just as decided as was that of others who suffered all the agony of a violent process."*[9]

"How wide the contrast between the course of Felix and that of the jailer of Philippi! The servants of the Lord were brought in bonds to the jailer, as was Paul to Felix. The evidence they gave of being sustained by a divine power, their rejoicing under suffering and disgrace, their fearlessness when the earth was reeling with the earthquake shock, and their spirit of Christlike forgiveness, sent conviction to the jailer's heart, and with trembling he confessed his sins and found pardon. Felix trembled, but he did not repent. The jailer joyfully welcomed the Spirit of God to his heart and to his home; Felix bade the divine Messenger to depart. The one chose to become a child of

37

God and an heir of heaven; the other cast his lot with the workers of iniquity."[10]

[1] Ellen G. White, *Steps to Christ,* p. 57.

[2] *Ibid.,* p. 26.

[3] ———, *Evangelism,* p. 284.

[4] *Ibid.,* p. 288.

[5] ———, *The Desire of Ages,* pp. 671, 672.

[6] ———, *Evangelism,* p. 295.

[7] *Ibid.*

[8] *Ibid.,* pp. 288, 289.

[9] *Ibid.,* pp. 287, 288.

[10] ———, *The Acts of the Apostles,* p. 426.

Chapter 6

Biblical Examples

Both the Old and New Testaments are filled with examples of different responses or reactions to the work of conviction. Consider these biblical illustrations.

Naaman the Leper

"So Naaman came with his horses and with his chariot, and stood at the door of the house of Elisha. And Elisha sent a messenger unto him, saying, Go and wash in Jordan seven times, and thy flesh shall come again to thee, and thou shalt be clean. But Naaman was wroth, and went away, and said, Behold, I thought, He will surely come out to me, and stand, and call on the name of the Lord his God, and strike his hand over the place, and recover the leper. Are not Abana and Pharpar, rivers of Damascus, better than all the waters of Israel? may I not wash in them, and be clean? So he turned and went away in a rage" (2 Kings 5:9-12). Fortunately for him, his servants gently yet logically appealed to his sense of reason. The resulting physical and spiritual restoration came after he laid aside his prideful rage and responded to heart conviction.

David

"And David said unto Nathan, I have sinned against the Lord. And Nathan said unto David, The Lord also hath put away thy sin; thou shalt not die" (2 Samuel 12:13). Immediate repentance was the king's response, accompanied by a willingness to accept the ensuing consequences of his own wrongdoing.

Nebuchadnezzar

"The king answered unto Daniel, and said, Of a truth it is, that your God is a God of gods, and a Lord of kings, and a revealer of secrets, seeing thou couldest reveal this secret" (Daniel 2:47). The king, being impressed by the conviction of new light, yielded to Daniel's humble revelation.

The Woman at the Well

Her conviction awakened when she stated, "Sir, I perceive that thou art a prophet" (John 4:19). Jesus then called for a *decision* to acknowledge Him as the Messiah (verse 21). She then jumped into an *action* appropriate to the decision (verse 28).

The Disciples

"Then they that were in the ship came and worshipped him, saying, Of a truth thou art the Son of God" (Matthew 14:33). Amazed at the miracle they had seen, they were compelled to render obeisance.

Rich Young Ruler

"And when he was gone forth into the way, there came one running, and kneeled to him, and asked him, Good Master, what shall I do that I may inherit eternal life? And Jesus said unto him, Why callest thou me good? there is none good but one, that is, God. Thou knowest the commandments, Do not commit adultery, Do not kill, Do not steal, Do not bear false witness, Defraud not, Honour thy father and mother. And he answered and said unto him, Master, all these have I observed from my youth. Then Jesus beholding him loved him, and said unto him, One thing thou lackest: go thy way, sell whatsoever thou hast, and give to the poor, and thou shalt have treasure in heaven: and come, take up the cross, and follow me. And he was sad at that saying, and went away grieved: for he had great possessions" (Mark 10:17-22). Though falling under conviction, he did not yield, because the cost required of him by Christ was greater than the desired want.

Peter

"And the Lord turned, and looked upon Peter. And Peter remembered the word of the Lord, how he had said unto him, Before the cock crow, thou shalt deny me thrice. And Peter went out, and wept bitterly" (Luke 22:61, 62). Peter was so stricken at the realization of his sin that the overwhelming conviction almost crushed him.

Jews on the Day of Pentecost

"Now when they heard this [Peter's preaching], they were pricked in their heart, and said unto Peter and to the rest of the apostles, Men and brethren, what shall we do? Then Peter said unto them, Repent, and be baptized every one of you in the name of Jesus Christ for the remission of sins, and ye shall receive the gift of the Holy Ghost" (Acts 2:37, 38). This powerful appeal stirred the hearts of the people and moved them to immediate action.

The Ethiopian Eunuch

"And the eunuch answered Philip, and said, I pray thee, of whom speaketh the prophet this? of himself, or of some other man? Then Philip opened his mouth, and began at the same scripture, and preached unto him Jesus. And as they went on their way, they came unto a certain water: and the eunuch said, See, here is water; what doth hinder me to be baptized? And Philip said, If thou believest with all thine heart, thou mayest. And he answered and said, I believe that Jesus Christ is the Son of God" (Acts 8:34-37). This man looked at the evidence and awoke to a new life.

Cornelius, the Roman Centurion

"And the morrow after, they entered into Caesarea. And Cornelius waited for them, and had called together his kinsmen and near friends. And as Peter was coming in, Cornelius met him, and fell down at his feet, and worshipped him. But Peter took him up, saying, Stand up; I myself also am a man. And as he talked with him, he went in, and found many that were come together" (Acts 10:24-27). The centurion was already under conviction, and so he responded by demonstrating a readiness to accept heaven's messenger.

The Roman Jailer

"Then he called for a light, and sprang in, and came trembling, and fell down before Paul and Silas, and brought them out, and said, Sirs, what must I do to be saved? And they said, Believe on the Lord Jesus Christ, and thou shalt be saved, and thy house" (Acts 16:29-31). The man's response here is obvious—the night's events had driven him to a point of instant conversion.

Through these examples one can readily see that not all responded alike. Some yielded to the Spirit's prompting; others completely rejected His leading. One responded with a positive attitude; others had violently negative reactions. "Some to whom conviction comes refuse to change their way of life, because to change would be an acknowledgment that they had been wrong. To them the conviction is useless. They do not allow it to work in them true reformation."[1] But irrespective of their final response, they were all impressed, and were free to choose their own course of direction. However, in most instances some individual served to aid the candidate to respond appropriately. In the case of Naaman, it was his servants. With David, it was the prophet. For the Jews of Pentecost, it was Peter moved by the Spirit to make an eloquent appeal. With the jailer, it was Paul's example of true conversion and Christlikeness while suffering abuse and injustice.

Here is found another important principle. Generally, a human agent must be involved in this process of decision. This duty is a divine privilege and a wonderful opportunity for all believers. Though God is entirely capable of accomplishing the work Himself, He delights in our participation. We are told, *"Everything that you can do to bring souls to a knowledge of the truth, is a means of allowing the light to shine, the light of the glory of God, as it shines in the face of Jesus Christ. Direct the mind to Him who guides and controls all things. Christ will be the manna and the spiritual dew to these newly converted souls. In Him is no darkness at all. As men of spiritual understanding conduct Bible studies with them, telling them how to yield to the power of the Holy Spirit, that they may be fully and firmly established in the truth, the power of God will be revealed."*[2]

"When the truth is preached, there should be wise, understanding workers, men and women who commune with God, who derive wisdom from the Source of all power, to make personal efforts for those who are under conviction."[3] "The teacher of truth is to take heed how he presents the truth. He is to speak every word plainly and distinctly, with that earnest conviction which carries conviction to hearts."[4] The early disciples "told their experience to the world with a confidence which carried with it the conviction that God was with them."[5] Their active role in seeking to win others is considered by heaven an essential element in the development of their own character. As the human agent recognizes their great privilege, they will seek more earnestly to cooperate with Christ.

"The souls under conviction of the truth need to be visited and labored for. Sinners need a special work done for them, that they may be converted and baptized."[6] "Let strong reasons for our faith be presented from the Word of God, and let the truth in its sanctifying power melt its way to the hearts and minds of those who are under conviction. As the helpers give Bible readings in the homes of the people, the Lord just as surely works on minds as He does in the public services."[7] If the Christian medical profession understood this concept as it should be, there would be far more conversions than there are now. The counsel is "Into the medical missionary work there must be brought more of a yearning for souls. It was this yearning that filled the hearts of those who established our first medical institution. Christ is to be present in the sickroom, filling the heart of the physician with the fragrance of His love. When his life is such that Christ can go with him to the bedside of the sick, there will come to them the conviction that He, the compassionate Saviour, is present, and this conviction will do much to restore them to health."[8]

---

[1] Ellen G. White, *Manuscript Releases,* vol. 6, p. 120.

[2] ———, *Evangelism,* p. 284.

[3] ———, *Manuscript Releases,* vol. 3, p. 15.

[4] ———, *The Voice in Speech and Song,* p. 39.

[5] ———, *The Acts of the Apostles,* p. 46.
[6] ———, *Evangelism,* pp. 306, 307.
[7] ———, *Ibid.,* p. 489.
[8] ———, *Medical Ministry,* p. 40.

Chapter 7

Examples of Various Indicators

Indications Through Anger

Let's examine a few examples of individuals and their different responses. This will aid us in getting a clearer grasp of these indicators and of how they reveal the presence of conviction. First, let's look at the indication of *anger*. Some time ago as I was holding a series of meetings in a church in Florida, I preached on the subject of Christian standards. At the conclusion of my meeting, Kathy, one of the participants, stopped me as I headed toward the exit. She was bubbling over with praise and thanksgiving for the message that had just been delivered. Exuberantly she expressed her appreciation for the deliverance she experienced through hearing the message.

Normally, when I finish speaking I make it a habit to go right to the back and greet the people as they are leaving. This gives me a chance to get a pulse on their response to the message. But this particular time I didn't have that luxury, as I remained listening to Kathy's testimony. When I finally arrived in the church foyer, my Bible worker exclaimed, "Whew! I'm so glad you didn't get out here sooner. Mrs. T was irate! She was out here pacing back and forth, waiting for you to come out so she could slap you in the face." To call Mrs. T angry was to understate the depth of her reaction significantly. Now, up to this point, she had been a very enthusiastic participant. Mrs. T had expressed to others how much she loved the messages. Not only had she attended every night, but she had brought her sister and brother-in-law, as well as her own husband. Now suddenly there was this change in her attitude. From the reaction my Bible worker had described, I knew that her anger was an evidence of strong conviction. Usually the stronger the conviction that takes hold, the stronger the reaction that is displayed.

"Well," I said, "I'll have to see her tomorrow." When I went to visit her the next day, her husband answered my knock. After explaining my desire to see his wife, he was incredulous.

"Are you crazy? Are you sure you want to come into my house?"

I told him, "Yes!"

He responded, "All right; you're on your own." He stepped aside to let me enter, and then made a hasty departure.

As soon she saw me she cried out with a snarling expression on her face, "You!" Then she proceeded to yell at me.

"What did I do?" I asked.

"How dare you embarrass me before all those people," she yelled back.

"How did I embarrass you?" I asked.

"You knew I was the only one with jewelry on!" she spat back.

"You were?" I questioned.

"You knew that!" she retorted.

Once she said that, I had concrete evidence that she was under the convicting power of God. When the Holy Ghost speaks to the heart, though they may be among a crowd of hundreds, the individual feels as if they are being singled out. So I continued to talk to her. "No, you were not the only one. There were many people in the audience wearing jewelry."

"There were?" she asked.

"Yes," I replied. "In fact, Mrs. J came up and told me how thankful she was for what I presented."

"She did?" Mrs. T questioned again.

"Yes, Mrs. J told me she had a chest full of jewelry.

In fact, she said to me, 'I'm so thankful for what you have shared. I loved jewelry, but until tonight I hadn't realized what a grip it has had on me. Now I see that the Lord is not pleased with my blind obsession for it. But I have a problem,' she continued. 'Just today my husband surprised me with a diamond necklace. Pray that God gives me wisdom to let him know that although I appreciate it, I am not going to wear it anymore.'"

Amazed at the other woman's response, Mrs. T said, "Are you kidding?"

I replied, "No; in fact, the reason I came was because I felt *you* were struggling. I am so thankful that God's Spirit is speaking to your heart." After I explained to her the working methods of the Holy Spirit, she sobered and finally calmed down. She realized that it was not a human instrument she was dealing with, but rather God Himself. Though she did not make a final decision during my meetings, she was baptized later on.

Mrs. T and Mrs. J reacted in completely opposite ways to the moving of the Spirit. One was glad; the other angry. It is here that another point needs to be emphasized. Most people are very unaware of the workings of God's Spirit. The common person on the street does not know anything about the process of conviction or, for that matter, that it even exists. In the Bible we find an excellent example illustrating this point. The book of Acts tells us a story of Paul encountering this. "And it came to pass, that, while Apollos was at Corinth, Paul having passed through the upper coasts came to Ephesus: and finding certain disciples, he said unto them, Have ye received the Holy Ghost since ye believed? And they said unto him, We have not so much as heard whether there be any Holy Ghost. And he said unto them, Unto what then were ye baptized? And they said, Unto John's baptism" (Acts 19:1-3). Notice that these were disciples—religious people. If they, being baptized with the baptism of repentance, did not know that there was any such thing as a Holy Ghost, what can be expected of those who are not religiously experienced? Like Nicodemus, they are completely devoid of the reality of the presence and working of God through His Spirit.

Consequently, when conviction strikes the heart and mind of a person, because of their ignorance they relegate it as being the fault of the human agent. This of course is the work of the devil. If he can lead the person to believe it to be the human instrument, then there is the possibility that the conviction can be discarded. Usually the victim interprets it as "guilt" or "being harassed" or "hounded." This is why it is so needful to recognize God's moving in the lives of others. If His presence is recognized, then at the appropriate time, the recipient can be educated concerning how God works on the human heart. Then they can be led or encouraged to do their part in yielding to and cooperating with His prompting.

It is extremely essential to educate the candidate on what is really taking place. By so doing, you can grasp that which the enemy of souls endeavors to make common, and place it back into the realm of the sacred. We must therefore labor to help the candidate understand that it is not the human agent, but rather the Lord, who is troubling their conscience. Let me cite another biblical example. Ahab, the wicked king of Israel, once said to the prophet Elijah, "Art thou he that troubleth Israel?" (1 Kings 18:17). He blamed the prophet for bringing him and his people to a level of consciousness that he and they were uncomfortable with. And while it is true that the faithful prophet was the instrument, it was God who was doing the convicting.

What is our role in this process? If we understand what is happening behind the scenes, we must participate in doing our part to help the candidate become aware of what is transpiring within their own hearts. We must teach them God's methods of speaking to the conscience. Candidates need to be led to an understanding of how He convicts, as well as the usual patterns of responses. It is needful to give them biblical examples on the Holy Spirit's labors with others and the given responses or reactions. They should be instructed concerning His role in our salvation. Once they have been led to recognize and accept these facts, there is a greater possibility that they will want to cooperate with God rather than fight against Him. If we are not present to do our part, there is great danger for the candidate. We are counseled, "As men of spiritual understanding conduct Bible studies with them, telling them how to yield to the power of the Holy Spirit, that they may be fully and firmly established in the truth, the power of God will be revealed."[1]

People's spiritual lives can be placed in jeopardy if they are left with the notion that it is you, the human agent, who is responsible for their trouble. If left to arrive at this erroneous conclusion, it becomes easier to reject the impressions of the Holy Spirit on the sinful heart. But if they can be led to understand that it is God who is at work, if they are truly sincere, they will be careful how they relate to their deepening sense of conviction. This will unveil to them the reality of the great controversy being played out for ownership of the human soul and will provide a stronger incentive to yield to the Lord.

Indications Through Avoidance

Now let's take "avoidance" as another example. I was holding a series of meetings in Roswell, New Mexico. A year earlier I had held my first meetings in the nearby town of Riodoso, baptizing three persons. At the Roswell meetings, one of the first three—who later became a Bible worker—encouraged several youth to attend. She was so excited with the message that she accompanied her hippie friends every night. At the time, my meetings were held every night of the week without pauses. In spite of the long drive, they came every night, 74 miles one way. Since I could not drive to visit them, they would stay up until midnight to ask questions before driving home. They would get up at 5:00 a.m., work until 5:00 p.m., then carpool to the meetings. Their sacrifices spoke volumes of their level of interest.

Among these youth there was an interesting young Pentecostal preacher named Allen. I discovered that his purpose in coming was to win these enthusiastic youths to his own religious persuasion. So he would accompany them to each message, then on the way back would proceed to contradict what I was teaching. But one night the message seemed to trouble him. Consequently, though he continued coming down with the group, he did not attend the meetings. Instead he would spend the evening across the street at a neighbor's house, and then would return home with the youth.

The first night he did that, I made a mental note of his absence. Everybody else was there except Allen. When I questioned the group concerning his whereabouts they responded, "Well, he didn't want to come in tonight."

"Where is he?" I asked.

"He's across the street."

Allen's absence continued for several nights, telling me that he was in the *avoiding* mode. So on the third night I told the group, "Let's go across the street. I must see him."

When we stepped up on the front porch, he didn't seem to be around. At our knock the lady of the house came out and whispered, "He's inside."

I decided to sit and wait on the porch. *He's going to have to come out sometime,* I thought. So I waited and waited and waited some more. He just wasn't going to come out while I was there. About midnight I heard a noise coming from the side of the house. Looking around the corner, I saw a man's leg protruding from the window. It was Allen, and he was sneaking through the window. He jumped out and proceeded running toward the backyard. Quickly I jumped over the banister and chased after him, keeping pace as he dodged around parked cars. Since he was a smoker, I knew he would have to give up running sooner or later. Finally he couldn't run anymore. By now he was panting. I walked up by his side. Acting surprised, as though he hadn't known that I was behind him, he said, "What are you doing here?"

"Allen, I just want you to understand one thing. You are not running from me. You are running from the Lord—God is the one speaking to you." He tried to argue. But I kept to the affirmative, and then encouraged him to ask God for a heart that was willing to surrender.

I found out later that Allen had a struggle before him. From childhood he had dreamed of becoming a minister. Now that his dream had become a reality, he feared that acceptance of these new teachings would force him to forgo his life's aspiration. He wasn't baptized during that series of meetings, but about a year later I received a telephone call at 2:00 in the morning. "Hey, guess who this is! It's Allen. I'm just calling to let you know that I am now a Seventh-day Adventist. I'm in Mexico doing missionary work on behalf of the church."

What was Allen's biggest obstacle? He felt conviction, but he was trying to avoid it. As far as he was concerned, it was the preacher who troubled him. It was my responsibility to clarify that deception in his mind—even though it meant chasing after him at someone else's house in the middle of the night. My point? You must be aware of the evidences of spiritual conviction. If the candidate is coming, coming, coming, and all of a sudden withdraws, don't think that he or she just isn't interested anymore. In this situation something is wrong, and the only safe course is to stick with the interested person until the problem can be resolved.

Remember, as you present the truth many problems will arise in people's minds. You may often be the recipient of their wrath. But don't take it personally—they are only reacting to the unknown. This is why it is so important for people who understand what is happening and know how to aid the troubled soul to help distressed candidates toward the step of surrender. People sometimes attempt to rationalize because of the inward struggles they encounter under the Spirit's influence. Often they are confronted with obstacles that appear insurmountable. The presence of someone with discernment and skill is crucial in these moments.

Right here I want to present another crucial point. When the Lord is working on the human heart, the devil is always there to confuse. Most of the time the enemy of souls uses people's ignorance against them. Here is an example from my own conversion experience. When I was a young musician I was first confronted with Christianity. I'd been performing with Bill Haley and the Comets and had returned home for a break. My brother had recently become a Seventh-day Adventist and began witnessing to me. The reality hit me that I needed to make a choice between God and my career. But the next thought that came to me was frightening: *If I become a Christian, I cannot have any fun.* Is this true? Christians typically answer, "No!" But it *is* true—if you look at it from my perspective. The only "fun" I knew was immorality, drugs, and the lifestyle that accompanies them. Of course, as a Christian I could not have this kind of fun. But since I did not know the true joy and clean fun that a Christian can have, I almost decided against following Christ. So it is with the sinner who is lost in sins and blinding transgressions. "Many have confused ideas as to what constitutes faith, and they live altogether below their privileges. They confuse feeling and faith, and are continually distressed and perplexed in mind; for Satan takes all possible advantage of their ignorance and inexperience."[2]

Indications Through Silence

Throughout my ministerial experience I have seen and encountered numerous variations of reaction to conviction. Here is another example, this time illustrating the silence indicator. I was holding meetings in Baltimore, and after the first week I went out on visitation, as is my custom. There was a young Black man attending the meetings, a very happy-go-lucky fellow. But during each message he was silent. When I visited his house, I noticed that on his living room floor were stacks of videos, but I didn't say anything about it. I just climbed over the stacks, sat down, and began to talk with him. At the appropriate time I asked, "By the way, what are you doing with all those videos on the floor?"

"Well," he said, "I can't watch these anymore."

His response was interesting. I had not talked about videos. Neither had I mentioned anything about the subject matter that concerned him. "Why?" I asked him.

"The Lord is not pleased with me watching those things," he replied.

Without realizing it, what did he reveal to me about his level of commitment? His response gave evidence that the regenerating power of the Holy Spirit was at work. When I heard him say those words, I knew that if he continued attending the meetings and kept responding to the voice of God, he would be baptized. And he was!

---

[1] Ellen G. White, *Evangelism,* p. 284.

[2] ———, *Our High Calling,* p. 77.

Chapter 8

The Spirit, Not the Tool, Does the Work!

In many congregations there have been attempts on the part of the clergy to get members involved in outreach and soul winning. Fearing that the members will shy away from anything too difficult, the pastors try to make it as easy as possible. They say something like "All you have to do is take this Dukane slide projector, place it in the right spot in the living room, and let the people watch. It's that simple!"

Generally the idea transmitted is that if the layperson is persistent enough and shows the videos or slides often enough, then the hearer will be converted. While this sometimes works (because of God's mercy for the lost), the majority of the time it doesn't. A disservice is done when the novice is led to depend on leading a soul to Christ by proxy. I repeat—the tool is not the one to do the work. The tool is created to *be* worked! The method cannot perform the job. An effort must be made to become connected heart-to-heart with individuals. A slide projector cannot detect the depth of emotion that the human eye can perceive. There must be a vigilant watching for conviction; sometimes it may strike at the second Bible study, not at the twenty-fourth! In other words, conviction may take hold when you least expect it. That is the way the Holy Spirit works. We cannot circumscribe the Holy

Spirit. When He decides to make the fruit ripe, we must be ready to pick it.

If the tendency is to depend upon the method or tool, a person is liable to think that their sole job is to guide the candidate through the 24 lessons. This places the burden on disseminating information. And while doctrinally correct information is imperative, it cannot replace the role of a caring human agent. This misguided concept of working for souls is one of the leading causes for today's widespread failure in personal witnessing. The unwary worker is waiting for the completion of the 24 lessons to call for a decision from the recipient. At the conclusion, the lay worker expects something miraculous to happen. But conviction may have struck at the fifth, sixth, or tenth lesson, then withered away unobserved. Because that sense of conviction is not immediately encouraged, it often dies. And by the time the lessons are finished, all that has taken place is an exchange of ideas that oftentimes fails to bear fruit.

There are many laypeople who go out to give Bible studies. They try to keep the person going until they finally finish the complete set of lessons. It is almost as if their consuming objective is merely to convince the students of doctrinal facts. But conversion does not come solely from feeding facts. In fact, in too many cases the interested person is led to accept facts without any conversion experience. These are they who most often become legalistic Christians. But if they don't accept the teachings, the scenario frequently ends up with the person saying, "Thanks so much. You have been so kind to me." To this the instructor says, "Oh well, I guess they weren't interested in the first place." But in reality that may not have been the case. The instructor must ask themselves deeper questions. What was I watching for?

What signals was I watching for? Was I able to pinpoint their moments of conviction?

If the instructor had known what to look for and was perceptive in their observations, they might have been able to pick up on the person's spiritual vital signs earlier on. Remember! You are watching for conviction! It can take place anytime, and when it does, you must be prepared to recognize it.

Haven't you heard of people, as they hear the Word of God, exclaiming, "Man, this is great!" Then they go to their friends and say, "Hey! Do you know we shouldn't do . . . ?" Their excitement compels them to tell others their new knowledge. They just can't keep the good news to themselves. When you visit their homes, they will exclaim, "This is tremendous! Where have I been? Why hasn't anyone told me this before?" As an intuitive instructor, what is that telling you? Is conviction present? Yes! And what is your ensuing responsibility? You must cultivate the seeds until you can reap the harvest. I have found that most failures on the part of people and training programs is that they misplace their emphasis. Students usually are not taught how to decipher, to discern if there is an attitude of avoidance, or to watch and see how the Spirit moves on hearts. Yet that is precisely what the worker must learn to do. Is the Spirit working? Is change taking place? If so, then you have results to look forward to. If no reaction is being stirred, don't try to draw the candidate toward a decision. There is no inner commitment to draw against.

An evangelist bought state-of-the-art equipment and then called me up to ask if he could hold a series of meetings for my church. He was excited about his new program and wanted the opportunity to try it out. When the meetings began, no one questioned that the equipment and the program was the latest. In fact, the preaching was canned, perfectly synchronized with slides. Night after night he continued. As we approached nearer the end of the meetings he verbalized his concern. No one was moving. There were no decisions, no commitments, no responses. Finally he demanded, "What do I do?"

"Preach!" I replied. "You have been depending on your beautiful program and the latest technology to do the work for you. But if you are going to gain any results, you will have to start preaching and making appeals."

He confessed he had banked his future success so fully on this approach that he had discarded all his sermons. I lent him mine, and he began to preach; several made their decisions and were baptized. Regrettably, many people are just like that evangelist. They have either never known or have lost the ability to detect evidences of the Spirit's moving.

On another occasion it was my responsibility to supervise and train evangelists. I went to visit a particular campaign. The evangelist was preaching forcibly. He had all his facts straight and most up-to-date statistics on current events. He had tremendous information. But he wasn't getting any decisions. Frustrated, he told me, "I don't know what is wrong. I think I am preaching it."

I said, "Yes, you're preaching it, but there is one element missing. You're not trying to reach the heart. As a result, conviction is not surfacing. If there is no conviction planted in the meeting hall, there will be nothing to cultivate in the home. Because of this lack, what you are not doing in the meetings is left to be accomplished in the home. There is just one problem. You have neither the same atmosphere nor the same length of time in someone's house that you have in the meeting place." Conviction must be created in the meeting hall, and once it is there, then you can pull for a decision. If there is no conviction, there will be no decision. And remember this: "Your success will not depend so much upon your knowledge and accomplishments, as upon your ability to find your way to the heart."[1]

The following day I went with this evangelist to visit some of his interests. As we visited, it became quite evident that they knew the information, but lacked the drive to follow it. There was no remorse for sin, no growth in grace, and no indication that God's Spirit was working. One individual said, "Boy, I had never heard anything like that before. But I don't have any plans to join a different church. I'm happy where I am."

"When somebody makes a statement like that, do you think there is any conviction present?" I asked the evangelist.

"No!" he said. And fortunately, he got the picture.

But with all the importance of accurately judging indicators, there is one added caution: Do not think that just because a person gets mad, they are under conviction. Don't assume that if you knock on a door and someone slams it back in your face, this equals conviction. However, if you have been working with that person and all of a sudden you see a change, what is present? Conviction! You're preaching the gospel, and as you are preaching, you see tears. What is present? Conviction! You see a face in your congregation light up. What is tugging at their heart? Conviction! Once you recognize the presence of conviction, then you must take action to bring the person to a positive decision. You must "strike while the iron is hot."

Strike While the Iron Is Hot!

With every soul there is a critical moment when it is essential for the soul winner to act. The following statement reinforces this fact. "Many are convicted of sin, and feel their need of a sin-pardoning Saviour; but they are merely dissatisfied with their pursuits and aims, and if there is not a decided application of the truth to their hearts, if the words are not spoken at the right moment, calling for a decision for the weight of evidence already presented, the convicted ones pass on without identifying themselves with Christ, the golden opportunity passes, and they have not yielded, and they go farther and farther away from the truth, farther away from Jesus and never take their stand on the Lord's side."[2] How important is it then to recognize conviction? Decision calls are not only necessary; they are critical. Therefore, if you are not recognizing and calling for decisions at the right moment, those people pass on. What a terrible thing!

Let's look at the rest of this statement. "When persons who are under conviction are not brought to make a decision at the earliest period possible, there is danger that the conviction will gradually wear away."[3] Consider the next quote. "It is as much our duty to look at the afterinterests [candidates] of a camp meeting as it is to look after the present interests, because the next time you go, if they were impressed and convicted, and did not yield to that conviction, it is harder to make an impression on their minds than it was before, and you cannot reach them."[4] The camp meeting that is here spoken about is an evangelistic meeting. In those days of camp meeting, people gathered together and undertook a spiritual assault on a city and its surrounding area. They would camp for several months just outside a city. They sent the "marines" (Christian literature salespeople) in first. The interests they found were handed over to the Bible workers for personal study. Finally, the evangelist came in last, preaching at the meeting series. When the meetings concluded, the team left a group of workers behind to follow up the interests. Why the follow-up? They knew the necessity of binding up the remaining interests who were still indecisive under conviction. If they didn't keep contact with these individuals, the next time truth was presented there was the danger that these could not be reached. This is why committed evangelists are always under the gun to get the decision "now." This understanding creates their sense of urgency when they see God moving in the lives of candidates.

Sadly, there are many in the churches that don't understand these things. They have never read these statements, and so they criticize the soul winner, assuming that the evangelist is just after numbers. Often I have had people of this mind-set stand in the way of evangelism, hindering effective ministry and outreach. While womb has broken its water, well-meaning yet ignorant church members involve themselves, trying to stop the birth process. Without realizing it, they are attempting to circumscribe the working of the Holy Spirit.

Think of the exasperating challenge this presents to the soul winner! All the signs of conviction are present. Perhaps the person is struggling, but you know time is of the essence. You know that you have to get a decision now; a soul is hanging in the balance of eternity. You are compelled to act. You plead with the soul as one who must give an account in heaven. Laboring against resistance from onlookers, you lead the person to make a decision, and they choose baptism. Because this new babe in Christ is born prematurely, the members of the church must incubate them. But since the general membership is not active in soul winning, they do not understand all the dynamics we have just mentioned. Since they do not act their part, since they provide no nurturing atmosphere, the new convert dies spiritually. And the usual response from those who never understood the process? They stand by and cast blame: "All he did was wet the candidate!"

It is not enough to proclaim the message or even to convince people that the doctrines are true. The entire purpose of preaching truth is to lead people to accept it. Our commission from the Lord is not merely to warn others, but to make disciples of all people, to make Christians. That means that, as a soul winner, I'm not just out to preach; I'm out to make disciples. "Ye have not chosen me, [said the Lord] but I have chosen you, and ordained you, that ye should go and bring forth fruit, and that your fruit should remain: that whatsoever ye shall ask of the Father in my name, he may give it you" (John 15:16). In the Great Commission Jesus declares, "All power is given unto me in heaven and in earth. Go ye therefore, and teach all nations, baptizing them in the name of the Father, and of the Son, and of the Holy Ghost: teaching them to observe all things whatsoever I have commanded you: and, lo, I am with you alway, even unto the end of the world. Amen" (Matthew 28:18-20). It is my duty to go and compel them to come in. It is the duty of God's Spirit to convert them.

---

[1] Ellen G. White, *Evangelism,* p. 437.

[2] *Ibid.,* p. 283.

[3] *Ibid.,* p. 229.

[4] *Ibid.,* p. 293.

Chapter 9

Do's and Don'ts of Decision-making

Once we have recognized the presence of conviction, it is crucial that we understand the do's and don'ts of guiding a person through the decision process. There are certain challenges that may seem formidable in the mind of the one experiencing conviction. These may serve as a discouragement and hindrance in advancement toward the final step. Hence, understanding how to keep the person constantly focusing their attention on what God can do and what He has done, giving evidence that it is God rather than the human agent calling, becomes paramount.

But before we discuss the nitty-gritty of these do's and don'ts, there is one other crucial element—the ability to "ask." Unless you ask for a decision, one will not be made. There are those who assume this should be left only to the Holy Spirit. But the example of Jesus and His followers on this point is worthy of our emulation. Jesus directly said, "Follow Me." In another place He bade the people, "Yet a little while is the light with you. Walk while ye have the light, lest darkness come upon you: for he that walketh in darkness knoweth not whither he goeth" (John 12:35).

Here Jesus is making an appeal for His hearers to move forward. His example dictates that it is not enough to present truth. There must be an injunction given, an appeal made to encourage forward movement. Jesus not only preached and lived this example, but He gave clear, explicit, and implicit communication that made plain what He expected from those who heard Him.

To Zacchaeus the crooked tax collector He said, "Zacchaeus, make haste, and come down; for to day I must abide at thy house" (Luke 19:5). The rich young ruler was not left in ambivalence, wondering what should be done concerning Jesus' teaching. To him He said, "Yet lackest thou one thing: sell all that thou hast, and distribute among the poor, and thou shalt have treasure in heaven: and come, follow me" (Luke 18:22).

The apostle Peter, who learned many things as he watched his Master work, obviously learned this concept well. Giving a classic example of the principle "strike while the iron is hot" when he was asked: "Men and brethren, what shall we do?" he responded, "Repent, and be baptized every one of you in the name of Jesus Christ for the remission of sins, and ye shall receive the gift of the Holy Ghost. For the promise is unto you, and your children, and to all that are afar off, even as many as the Lord our God shall call. And with many other words did he testify and exhort, saying, Save yourselves from the untoward generation" (Acts 2:37-40). The response to his asking was marvelous. The Scripture record states, "Then they that gladly received his word were baptized: and the same day there were added unto them about three thousand souls" (verse 41).

Initially you may be uncomfortable with this thought. But if you are going to get a decision, you must *ask for it!* Many souls stay uncommitted, many decisions remain unmade, simply because no one has called for them.

I once worked with an intern who did not believe soul winning was his calling. Though he was unwilling, I persuaded him to hold a series of meetings. He went, despite thinking it was an effort in futility. Toward the end of the meetings I visited just to see how he was doing. He preached a very moving message. As I observed the audience, people were visibly moved. I expected a call from the pulpit, but none was made. When everyone was gone, I asked him a question. "Bob, why didn't you make a call?"

"For what?" he retorted.

"There were several folk under conviction. I thought if you had made a call, you would have had several decisions!" I responded.

"Where?" he questioned.

After I named a few, he agreed.

"Then why didn't you make an appeal?" I continued.

"I was afraid to ask, because I didn't know if anyone would respond. I didn't want to look foolish."

"Tomorrow I'll be here again," I informed him. "I want you to make an appeal then."

"What?" he didn't sound enthusiastic. "I don't know how to make an appeal."

"I will write out the appeal," I comforted him. "All you have to do is read it. If it doesn't work, I'll take the responsibility for the results."

"All right," he agreed nervously.

The next night I visited again. Again he preached a tremendous message. But when it came to the moment of appeal, he acted like a novice pilot trying to land during his first flight lesson. He came right to the point, but at the last moment he got scared and moved away from the subject. As I began to pray he came to the appeal again. But once more he skirted it and shifted away.

"Lord," I prayed, "help him to make it." Feeling somewhat uneasy, he finally arrived at the right point again. This time he decided to plunge in, even if it meant a crash landing. As he blurted out the appeal, his nervousness turned to amazement as four people responded, making decisions to be baptized. Bob was moved to tears. He had gained his first candidates for the kingdom!

Bob learned a very precious lesson through that ordeal. He discovered that there are souls being worked upon by the Spirit, but decisions for truth are seldom made unless they are called for. Bob was never the same after that experience. In fact, when he was placed in his first pastoral district, he was there only a few weeks before he asked to borrow my equipment again to hold his own series of meetings for his churches. In giving that first prewritten appeal, Bob had gotten a taste for soul winning. But more than this, he was able to see the essential aspect of being brave enough to "ask."

Fear seems to paralyze many. But let's address this crippling sensation often experienced in those who, but for this problem, would otherwise be a power for good. This young pastor, Bob, though very talented was hindered because of this weakness. And so it is with many a pastor and layperson. Consider this statement: "When souls are first converted to the truth, they should be instructed as to what Christ expects from them in living, wholehearted service—that He invites them to be laborers in His moral vineyard. *However trembling may be their efforts, however imperfect their work, they should be patiently and lovingly borne with; for if they are meek and lowly in heart, the Lord can turn what appears to be defeat, into signal victory.* Every soul born of the Spirit of God is to grow up into Christ, the living head. Under apprenticeship to Christ, those who profess His name are to become apt scholars, learning how to cooperate with heavenly intelligences in drawing souls to

Christ. To every one the Lord has given His work."[1]

We must trust not in what "I can accomplish," but rather in what God can do! "God can and will use those who have not had a thorough education in the schools of men. A doubt of His power to do this is manifest unbelief; it is limiting the omnipotent power of the One with whom nothing is impossible. *O for less of this uncalled-for, distrustful caution! It leaves so many forces of the church unused; it closes up the way, so that the Holy Spirit cannot use men; it keeps in idleness those who are willing and anxious to labor in Christ's lines; it discourages from entering the work many who would become efficient laborers together with God, if they were given a fair chance."*[2]

There is no question that the possibility is always present for people not to respond to either a personal appeal or a public appeal. Jesus Himself had to experience rejection, but this in no way deterred Him from making appeals either in a public forum or on the personal level. He realized the principle that "those who are seeking for truth need to have words spoken to them in season; for Satan is speaking to them by his temptations. If you meet with repulse when trying to help souls, heed it not. If there seems to be little good resulting from your work, do not become discouraged. Keep working; be discreet; know when to speak, and when to keep silent; watch for souls as they that must give an account; and watch for the devices of Satan, lest you be led aside from duty. Do not allow difficulties to dishearten or intimidate you. With strong faith, with intrepid purpose, meet and overcome these difficulties. Sow the seed in faith, and with an unsparing hand."[3]

This problem is not limited to us today. The prophets of old also suffered from this challenge. Let me say that it is OK to fear. It is fear that enables us to avoid danger, to heed warnings and escape. Because of the sinful condition on this earth we recognize the importance of teaching our children fear and precaution. The Word of God itself teaches us that the fear of God is the beginning of wisdom. Notice this statement: "'Let us therefore fear, lest, a promise being left us of entering into his rest, any of you should seem to come short of it' . . . The Lord would have His people trust in Him and abide in His love, but that does not mean that we shall have no fear or misgivings. Some seem to think that if a man has a wholesome fear of the judgments of God, it is a proof that he is destitute of faith; but this is not so. A proper fear of God, in believing His threatenings, works the peaceable fruits of righteousness, by causing the trembling soul to flee to Jesus. Many ought to have this spirit today, and turn to the Lord with humble contrition, for the Lord has not given so many terrible threatenings, pronounced so severe judgments in His word, simply to have them recorded, but He means what He says. One says, 'Horror hath taken hold upon me because of the wicked that forsake thy law.' Paul says, 'Knowing therefore the terror of the Lord, we persuade men.'"[4]

From this statement we can see that it is all right to fear. Fear is an element necessary in this landmine-ridden earth in which we live. But how you direct your fear is what makes a difference in your level of effectiveness. To one extent or another, most public speakers have a certain level of apprehension, but through experience they have learned to direct that energy to bring positive outcomes.

We can see from Jeremiah's experience that he feared. However, he determined to obey the voice of the Lord rather than the voice of fear. Notice his experience. "Then the word of the Lord came unto me, saying, Before I formed thee in the belly I knew thee; and before thou camest forth out of the womb I sanctified thee, *and* I ordained thee a prophet unto the nations. Then said I, Ah, Lord God! behold, I cannot speak: for I *am* a child." Let's look at God's response to him. "But the Lord said unto me, Say not, I *am* a child: for thou shalt go to all that I shall send thee, and whatsoever I command thee thou shalt speak. Be not afraid of their faces: for I *am* with thee to deliver thee, saith the Lord. Then the Lord put forth his hand, and touched my mouth. And the Lord said unto me, Behold, I have put my words in thy mouth. See, I have this day set thee over the nations and over the kingdoms, to root out, and to pull down, and to destroy, and to throw down, to build, and to plant" (Jeremiah 1:4-10).

Moses' story is a poignant example in the overcoming of fear. He openly expressed to God his lack of confidence in his ability to fulfill the call presented before him. Once a man who had been trained in the royal Egyptian courts, he was now timid and uncertain of himself. When God spoke to him, he replied, "Who am I, that I should go unto Pharaoh, and that I should bring forth the children of Israel out of Egypt?" (Exodus 3:11). Later on, after encouragement from God, he was still fearful of what other people would think of his efforts, and felt that he was the wrong person for the job. "Behold," he said, "they will not believe me, nor hearken unto my voice: for they will say, The Lord hath not appeared unto thee. . . . O Lord, I am not eloquent, neither heretofore, nor since thou hast spoken unto thy servant: but I am slow of speech, and of a slow tongue" (Exodus 4:1-20). Even with all of Moses' remonstrations against what he was being chosen to do, God gave him promises to encourage him toward his new duty. "Now therefore go," the Lord said to him, "and I will be with thy mouth, and teach thee what thou shalt say" (verse 12)

Remember, "God hath not given us the spirit of fear; but of power, and of love, and of a sound mind" (2 Timothy 1:7).

[1] Ellen G. White, in *The Home Missionary,* Sept. 1, 1892.

[2] ———, *Christian Service,* p. 24.

[3] ———, *Gospel Workers,* pp. 188, 189.

[4] ———, in *Review and Herald,* Oct. 21, 1890.

Chapter 10

Getting
the Decision

Obtaining the decision to accept Christ is not terribly difficult if the worker has been consistently attentive and observant. In this observation attention has been given to the developing spiritual growth in the person. It would be well at this point to separate the venues between a person in a public meeting and one working through an in-home Bible study. If you are having a series of meetings, sooner or later an appeal must be made. If an invitation to accept Christ is extended to those present, then it should be expected that those who respond desire to make a decision illustrating that acceptance. However, it should not be taken for granted that the individual understands or knows how to accept Christ. Many a person who responds to a public appeal does so out of the convicting sense that they need Christ in their lives. But even though they sense the tug of Christ on their hearts, and they even arrive at the altar weeping, they usually do not understand the part they have to play in the process of decision. Here is where the worker plays a major role. When a public appeal is going to be made, the speaker and/or the evangelistic team members should be ready with decision cards on their persons. As the people begin to respond to the appeal and either go to the front or stand or raise their hands, these cards should be placed in their hand immediately after they have responded.

As the individuals come forward, these "response cards" should be ready to give to each person. The cards should list several statements giving the respondent an opportunity to indicate the details of their commitment, and have a place for their name and other pertinent details.

For example:

1. I desire to accept Christ as my personal Saviour.

2. I desire to be baptized after the example of my Lord.

3. I have some problems to overcome; please pray for me.

4. I would like a visit from the pastor.

After explaining to the respondents the need to indicate their decision on the cards, collect them. Be sure to offer a short prayer for these and then dismiss them. At the appropriate time and place each card should be evaluated to determine the decision of each candidate.

Suppose the individual marks number one. It is essential that the worker make an appointment to visit the candidate as soon as possible. As you arrive at their home, keep in mind that you are going there for a specific purpose—to lead that individual through the process of accepting Christ as their Saviour.

After you have exchanged the usual greeting, get right to the point. With your Bible in hand, sit so that you can look at your candidate. You might say, "John, I was excited last night as you responded to the Lord in the appeal." (This affirmation is very important. You want to make sure the person understands that his response was to God's call, and not to that of the speaker.) "I noticed that you marked number one on the decision card. So I have come to help you. May we have a word of prayer?" (Make the prayer brief but directed at the intended purpose.) The prayer may say: "Dear Lord, thank You for the desire

Mary has to accept You as her Saviour. Please bless us as we take the time to draw near to You. In Jesus' name, Amen." If the candidate has a Bible, then you can say, "Turn with me to Revelation 3." (Give the person time to find their Bible. If they do not have one, let them read from yours.) "Now let's look at verse 20. Would you read that for me?"

"'Behold, I stand at the door, and knock: if any man hear my voice, and open the door, I will come in to him, and will sup with him, and he with me.'"

After the person reads the text, say: "Notice it says, 'I stand at the door and knock.' The question is Who is knocking?" (Let the candidate respond.) Usually they will answer, "The Lord."

You respond with "That's right!" Then you may ask, "Why is He knocking?" If your candidate answers, "Because He wants to come in!" you can affirm the correct answer. If the candidate does not get the point of the question, then clarify the point for them.

Now you can say, "When I came to your home, I knocked on the door. When you heard the knock, you looked through your window to see who was there. Here is an important question. Does your seeing, or recognizing, that I am there permit me entrance into your home?"

Wait for a response. Usually they will say, "No."

Then you comment, "That's how it is with many people. They believe God is there, but that is as far as it goes. If you were to ask people whether they believe in God, the majority will answer 'Yes.' But believing God is there is not sufficient. Notice that God desires more than just recognition. John 15:5 tells us 'I am the vine, ye are the branches.' If the Lord is to enter your heart, what must you do besides acknowledging that He is there?"

Again wait for the response. "Open the door," they may say.

"Yes, that is correct," you affirm. "There are many who have opened the door; they have a desire for God. Inwardly they wish they could know Him. But unfortunately, just having a desire is not sufficient; it does not permit entrance. I have knocked on the doors of too many homes where the door was opened, but I was not able to go in.

"So if the Lord is to enter, what must you do?" If the answer is correct, you then say, "Yes, that's right. You must invite Him in! The Lord never forces His way in. He waits for our invitation." The next question to ask is "Is there anything that would keep you from inviting Him into your heart?" At this time you must give the individual time to reflect. You have been walking them through a process of evaluating their motives. That's why the great question must be asked at this time. Once the question is posed it is important to give the individual time to answer. If the person says, "Nothing," then you invite him or her to kneel with you. At this time you encourage the individual to make the invitation. Let the person know that you will pray after he or she does. If the person says, "I don't know what to say," then ask, "What did you say in order for me to come into your home? It is that simple. The Lord would prefer that you expressed the intent of your heart." Then give him or her an opportunity to proceed.

Let's suppose that when the question "What would keep you from giving your heart?" is asked, the person says, "I have a smoking problem." You then need to ask if he or she feels the need to overcome. If the answer is affirmative, then you must pose the question: "Have you tried to quit before, without success?" If the answer is "Yes," then the next question is a key. "Can you quit through your own strength without the Lord?" If the answer is "No," then you must bring to their attention the reality that only through the Lord will they be able to find freedom. Since that is the case, you must return again to the question. "Is there anything that will keep you now?" If the answer is now "No," then proceed with the prayer of invitation.

Most of the time this is a very moving experience for the person. You have brought this individual face to face with the Lord, and now he or she is making a transition that will lead him or her into a saving relationship with Christ. It is essential that you seal the decision with prayer. Once the person prays, it is important for you to express your joy and gratitude for this moment in his or her life. You should offer thanksgiving for the decision made. The individual must be led to sense that this new commitment is between himself or herself and God. It is also imperative to express in your prayer the need for the person to grow in the knowledge of his or her Lord and Saviour. You never want to leave the individual with the impression that this now makes him or her perfect—that he or she is born into a fully grown character. No, no! You want the person to understand that he or she is born to continue growth.

Once you have finished praying together, a handshake or a hug (depending on the person and the situation) is in order. It is time to communicate your excitement over the individual's decision. You must go, but you want to leave him or her alone with the Lord. Once a person has made this decision, the next steps are to help him or her grow in knowledge of truth and in a deeper relationship with the Lord until he or she is ready for baptism. Remember, make sure you do not remain for any social activity. You want to leave the person in that solemn atmosphere.

Chapter 11

Public Calls

Let us address public calls. Making public calls or appeals is as critical as pulling in the line once the fish is hooked or gathering the fruit when it is ripe. The following statements underscore the importance of this element of preaching. "At the close of every meeting, decisions should be called for."[1] "For the secret of our success and power as a people advocating advanced truth will be found in making direct, personal appeals to those who are interested, having unwavering reliance upon the Most High."[2]

"The love of God in the heart [of ministers] will lead them to make earnest appeals—to warn, entreat, and reprove. If this work is neglected, souls will continue in sin, confirmed in a wrong course by those who have spoken to them only smooth things."[3] "In every discourse, fervent appeals should be made to the people to forsake their sins and turn to Christ."[4] "The people should be urged to decide just now to be on the Lord's side."[5]

There is a caution, however, that needs to be addressed. Do not treat an appeal or call as some addendum to your real message. The whole message must be structured as an appeal to the heart. Then and only then can a call for decision be truly effective. Do all that you can to treat every subject as an appeal to understand truth as it is in Jesus, as it relates to practical godliness. With your own heart filled with the convicting power of the Holy Spirit, strive to guide your listeners to a desire to follow your blessed Saviour in whatever the truth may be, however doctrinal or prophetic the subject matter. As you do this, an appeal or call will follow naturally.

There are also extremes to shun.

1. "Shunning to declare the whole counsel of God" (Acts 20:27).[6] Sometimes we think that if people are told the whole truth it will serve to discourage the candidate. It is true that you don't want to bring a person to the level of "information saturation." Neither do you want to preempt yourself—that is, giving information before candidates are ready to receive it. However, you do not want to mislead individuals by short-changing them. There are more than a few cases in which persons have been led to think that they are being baptized only in Christ, only to discover on their day of baptism that they are joining an organized church. This approach leads these people to feel they have been tricked.

2. "Weaving into the labors an element which moves the feelings and leaves the heart unchanged."[7] Feelings will be moved when the work is properly done in harmony with divine principles. But too often there is the danger that we can manipulate the feelings while leaving the life without the power-changing influence of the Holy Ghost. "A sensational religion is to be dreaded, for it is hard work, when once it has been woven into the experience, to ever make the individuals feel that they must go deeper than mere emotional exercise; that they must practice true godliness."[8]

3. "Hammering at the people in a harsh, unChristlike manner or talking in a way that they think you are provoked."[9] When you are calling for a decision, the use of spiritual intimidation or of verbal force will never accomplish what the Holy Spirit is able do. We need to manifest the compassion, tenderness, and the loving spirit of Christ!

Creating an Atmosphere of Conviction

As I have already stated, watch, watch! Remember, "every fresh display of the conviction of the grace of God upon the souls of unbelievers is divine."[10] "You should watch and see if there is an interest in this one or that."[11] As a young pastor, my focus was mostly centered on the preciseness and accuracy of my content and delivery. But as my experience deepened, I discovered that more important than my correctness was my need to concentrate on watching for the moving of the Holy Spirit on the hearts of my hearers. "As you present testing truth, [we are told] ask often, who is now willing, as they have heard the words of God, pointing out their duty, to consecrate their hearts and minds, with all their affections, to Christ Jesus."[12]

The love of Christ must have a part in every discourse!

1. There must be "a practical application . . . to their hearts."[13]

2. Make "earnest appeals that will reach their hearts."[14]

As you preach, watch for the response of the hearers. It is said of Christ, "He spoke directly to every mind and appealed to every heart. He watched the faces of His hearers, marked the lighting up of the countenance, the quick, responsive glance, which told that truth had reached the soul."[15] "Jesus watched with deep earnestness the changing countenances of His hearers. . . . As the arrows of truth pierced to the soul, breaking through the barriers of selfishness, and working contrition, and finally gratitude, the Saviour was made glad."[16]

As a speaker is delivering a message, "he will not dismiss a congregation without presenting before them Jesus Christ, the sinner's only refuge, making earnest appeals that will reach their hearts."[17] I have known some who are afraid to follow this counsel. One told me, "What if I make an appeal and no one responds? I'm afraid I will stand there looking silly." These fears keep many from becoming effective in their public speaking. However, if one makes only insipid entreaties, ineffectiveness is what can mostly be expected. But if we learn how to communicate earnest appeals, those fears will become mere unrealized anticipations.

In order to make heart-moving appeals, one must "cultivate earnestness and positiveness in addressing the people."[18] There may be those who, after reading this statement, remain convinced that this is not part of their personality. Maybe that is where the root of the problem lies. There are those who will take a "spiritual inventory test" to determine their gifts, or talents. Once they take the test they rely on the results to dictate their static abilities. But let's consider these thoughts: "Do not wait until some human examination pronounces you competent to work, but go out into the highways and hedges, and begin to work for God."[19] "God can and will use those who have not had a thorough education in the schools of men. A doubt of His power to do this is manifest unbelief; it is limiting the omnipotent power of the One with whom nothing is impossible. O for less of this uncalled-for, distrustful caution! It leaves so many forces of the church unused; it closes up the way, so that the Holy Spirit cannot use men; it keeps in idleness those who are willing and anxious to labor in Christ's lines; it discourages from entering the work many who would become efficient laborers together with God, if they were given a fair chance."[20]

Listen! "As the will of man cooperates with the will of God, it becomes omnipotent. Whatever is to be done at His command, may be accomplished in His strength. All His biddings are enablings."[21]

If God has commanded, "Go ye and preach," then it is not a test that determines our abilities, but rather the word of God. If you put your trust in His commands, then you will be able to preach and make appeals. "The reason why there is so little strength among those who profess the truth is that they do not exercise the ability that God has given them. Very many have wrapped their talent in a napkin and hid it in the earth. It is by using the talents that they increase."[22] "Your talents will increase by winning souls to Christ."[23] "We are to appreciate them [talents] as the gift of God, to cultivate and improve them, and place them at the service of God. This was the purpose for which talents were committed to us according to our ability to trade upon and cultivate those gifts. As we use our powers, we shall increase our ability to use them, and thus be enabled to do the highest kind of service. We shall be able to put our talents to a wise use; but if we do not use those qualifications of mind and body that God has given, however precious they may be, they will become valueless."[24]

To be successful in any field, one must apply the rules that have been proved to lead to success. If you are not personally moved by the message you present, it will be hard to move others toward a positive appeal response. "Your subject matter may be excellent, and just what the people need, but you would do well to mingle a positiveness with persuasive entreaties."[25] "Let your preaching be short and right to the point, and then at the proper time call for a decision. Do not present the truth in a formal manner, but let the heart be vitalized by the Spirit of God, and let your words be spoken with such certainty that those who hear may know that the truth is a reality to you." [26]

Though making public appeals may seem frightening to a speaker who is attempting it for the first time, it is really not that difficult. If the Lord has placed you in the position to deliver a message, then the appeal should not be made as though you are the one inviting, but rather as though you are God's mouthpiece. He is the one calling, not you. With this confidence, you have the freedom to appeal directly to the hearts of your hearers.

While you are making your appeal, here are a few points to remember. I believe these following points are necessary to an appeal's power. Some may consider them perfunctory, but they are the elements that will make or break the appeal. Let us consider these three essential elements to making a successful public appeal. Bear in mind that they must become an integral part of your thought process as you launch each appeal.

1. What: *What am I asking these people to do?* You have presented the message. What do you want them to do with it? If the subject was on heaven, will you invite them to want to be there?

2. How: *How am I telling them to indicate their response?* Are they to raise their hand, stand, walk forward to the altar, or fill out a decision card? You must make the response action clear. Otherwise, the people will be left frustrated, unsure how you expect them to respond.

3. When: *At what point during the appeal am I requesting them to show their response?* Example: "Oh, friend, isn't it time for you to give your heart fully to Jesus? If that is your desire, would you raise your hand now, just where you are?

Here are two "sample" calls. The first is a general call. The second is a specific call, ending with a general call in the event the speaker feels it is appropriate. God bless as you work to make your messages as appealing as possible under the guidance of the Holy Spirit!

General Call (to Be Used After "Heaven" Presentation)

"What a *marvelous* place heaven is! I want *so* much to be there.

"Wouldn't you like to raise your hand with me to say 'Yes, I too want to be there.' Is that your desire? [Raise your own hand.] Yes, just raise your hand right now. [Go directly into prayer with your hand raised.]

"Father, You see our hands raised. Please help us to keep our priorities straight. And help each one of us to be ready to live with You so we may realize this desire of our hearts. We look forward to this experience. Thank You for making all this possible through Jesus Christ our Lord. Amen."

Specific Call (to Be Used After a Major Message, Such as "The Mark of the Beast")

"To some of you, this message has come as a real shock. You may need time to study it out thoroughly and pray to God for strength to follow His revealed Word. But for others here tonight, this comes as a wonderful revelation, the missing piece of the puzzle, the light that clearly reveals the pathway of God. You hear God's voice speaking to you saying: 'My son, My daughter, will you stand on My side? Will you stand up for truth? Will you commit your life to being an example of pure religion, undefiled by human inventions and traditions?'

"Friend, if you hear *God's* voice *calling* you, will you just stand to your feet and be counted on His side right now?"

1. [If there is an immediate response] "God bless you

"Are there others? Yes, God bless you.

"Are there still others who are ready to take your stand with Jesus?

"We'll wait and pray. [Pause in attitude of prayer.]

"Are there others? Thank God." [Now go into prayer or move to your general appeal.]

2. [If no quick response] "I know that this is a very serious decision. A lot is at stake. The question each one of us must answer is Is this what Jesus wants? Is this His way? And if it is, friend, He is faithful. He will help you; He will guide you. He will strengthen you. But you must make the decision.

"Is there one who is ready to say: 'Yes Lord, here I am. You can count on me'?

"If you are that one, will you just stand where you are?"

[If there is a response, you should go back to number 1. If there is still no response, go on to the general appeal.]

General Appeal

"There are two other groups I want to include in this appeal.

"Because of the serious nature of this message, there are perhaps *those who do not have, just now, the strength to make this commitment* but who want to ask God for special help. *This is the first group.*

"The second group, I am sure, includes many of you. There are those here tonight who have previously committed their lives to live fully in harmony with God's revealed will but tonight your hearts have again been strangely warmed and you would like to say, 'Lord, You can count me in—I still pledge to stand for You and for Your truth.'

"If you are in either of these two groups—you need strength to stand, or you would like to recommit your life to God and His truth—would you join me in standing for Jesus?" [If some responded before, then say, "Would you join these who are standing now?"]

Prayer

"Father, here we stand, an army of Your children. Prepare us for combat, but even more, Father, prepare us for victory!

"You know, there are those standing here tonight who do not yet have the strength to move forward in Your truth. O God, come close to them. Guide their thinking, encourage their fainting hearts, and we will give You the praise and glory.

"And those who for the first time have stood in response to such a challenge, please keep them faithful and give them the strength of purpose that they need to move ahead with Christ from victory to victory.

"When You come, Father, and may it be soon, may we *all*—every person here tonight—be found faithful to You and ready to meet You in peace is my prayer in Jesus' name. Amen."

Sample Appeal Phrases
(These Are Some Thought Provokers!)
1. Will you be ready?
2. This is God's plan. Will you let Him include you?
3. What a beautiful message of hope. Do you have this hope?

Make a list of your own appeal phrases as you listen to others speak, and spend personal time with God's Word.

[1] Ellen G. White, *Testimonies for the Church,* vol. 6, p. 65.
[2] ————, in *Review and Herald,* Aug. 30, 1892.
[3] ————, *Gospel Workers* (1892), pp. 448, 449.
[4] ————, *Evangelism,* p. 280.
[5] Ellen G. White letter 29, 1890.
[6] Ellen G. White, *Evangelism,* p. 281.
[7] *Ibid.*
[8] ————, *Manuscript Releases,* vol. 17, p. 101.
[9] ————, *Evangelism,* p. 281.
[10] *Ibid.,* p. 284.
[11] *Ibid.,* p. 285.
[12] *Ibid.*
[13] *Ibid.,* p. 280.
[14] *Ibid.*
[15] ————, *Education,* p. 231.
[16] ————, *Evangelism,* p. 295.
[17] *Ibid.,* p. 280.
[18] *Ibid.,* p. 296.
[19] ————, *Testimonies for the Church,* vol. 7, p. 281.
[20] ————, *Christian Service,* p. 24.
[21] ————, *Christ's Object Lessons,* p. 333.
[22] ————, *Testimonies for the Church,* vol. 3, p. 57.
[23] ————, *Testimonies to Southern Africa,* p. 65.
[24] ————, in *Youth's Instructor,* Feb. 6, 1896.
[25] ————, *Evangelism,* p. 296.
[26] *Ibid.*

Chapter 12

Gaining Decisions for the Truth

The following is a list of the things that should not be done when you are seeking a decision. The "do not" list is just as important as the "must do" list. Heeding these will aid you in avoiding some of the typical pitfalls that others have fallen into when approaching candidates for a decision.

1. Do not proceed without heart preparation and prayer. This is a spiritual matter. Therefore, do not attempt to gain a decision without the assurance that the Lord is with you.

2. Do not condemn a person's past life. Give hope for the future. During one of my evangelistic meetings, a man who had just been driving by walked into my tent meeting. He looked like the famous Mr. Clean caricature from TV commercials—handlebar mustache, bald head, rippling muscles, and all. On the third night I made an appeal. This hulk of a man came forward weeping. After I dismissed the audience, he and his wife waited to talk with me.

"Can God forgive me?" he asked.

"Yes! God can forgive anyone."

"But you don't understand," he retorted. "You don't know what I have done."

"Then tell me what you have done," I said.

"I have killed 3,500 people." He spoke sadly of his time in Vietnam.

What do you do when a person has relished killing that many people? You must give them hope for the future! So I shared with him the promise in 1 John 1:9: "If we confess our sins, he is faithful and just to forgive us our sins, and to cleanse us from all unrighteousness."

He asked, "Can this be true?"

I assured him it was. We both knelt, and with tears streaming down his face he begged for forgiveness and claimed the promise of God.

3. Don't lose your temper or argue. If you lose your temper or argue, you will leave the impression that you are the one they are dealing with instead of God. You must never bring the gospel down to a common level.

4. Don't interrupt a person who is raising an honest objection. His opinion is important to him. Treat all objections as honest ones, unless otherwise determined. I once visited a husband whose Christian wife had begged me to see him. He had been faithfully attending my meetings. At the beginning of the visit I asked his wife to please give us privacy. (Often resistant spouses need to be able to express themselves without the presence of the one they have been standing against.) After the usual greetings I thanked him for attending my meetings, and asked if he was enjoying them.

"Yes," he responded.

"How long have you been a member?" I asked, though I knew he was not.

"I am not," he replied.

"Oh," I said. "Have you been baptized?"

"Yes!" he said.

"When?" I inquired.

"When I was a baby, of course."

"Oh, so you must have repented," I returned.

"Repented?" he retorted.

"Yes, the Bible says, 'Repent and be baptized.'"

"But I was too young to have known anything. Besides, I don't need to be baptized. The thief on the cross was not baptized, and Jesus promised him eternal life."

"What does the Bible say?" I questioned. Turning to John 3, I read aloud, "'Jesus answered and said unto him, Verily, verily, I say unto thee, Except a man be born again, he cannot see the kingdom of God. Nicodemus saith unto him, How can a man be born when he is old? can he enter the second time into his mother's womb, and be born? Jesus answered, Verily, verily, I say unto thee, Except a man be born of water and of the Spirit, he cannot enter into the kingdom of God'" (verses 3-5).

He was silent.

"Don, are you having problems with a sin, such as smoking or drinking?" I asked.

"Oh, no!" he responded.

"Is there some sin that you are hiding?" I persisted.

"No!" he said.

I had done my diagnostic questioning. He didn't smoke. He paid his tithe, believed in the Bible, and attended church on the Sabbath. *What could be holding him back?* I thought. "Don, are you afraid of water?" I finally asked.

"Who told you that?" He was surprised.

That was the problem! Don then confessed that as a child, he had been caught in a flood. His near-death experience with water terrified him to the point that he was paranoid of even a full bathtub. Working out this problem and helping him overcome his paranoia through prayer and Bible promises gave him the victory. On the day of his baptism it was obvious by his shaking robe that he was going against all his trepidations. Breaking the water as he was raised up from baptism, he exclaimed, "Wooo! If I had known it was this easy, I would have done it a long time ago." Don died a year later. I thank God he made his decision just in time.

5. Don't adopt a "that's nothing compared with . . ." attitude toward a person's problems. Remember, it is the one who stirs the kettle who knows what is in it. In other words, the heaviness of a burden is determined by the one carrying it. Therefore, consider every challenge as needing the help of the Omnipotent. Acknowledge the person's problem. Then with the help of the Lord, guide the candidate toward a solution.

6. Don't be impatient with a person who appears to respond too slowly. I labored and prayed for one of my brothers for 25 years. The long efforts and patience paid off. He was finally baptized.

7. Don't use the "take it or leave it" approach. God never has said, "If you don't want it, then leave it." On the contrary, His offer is always "Take it."

8. Try not to pull the candidate faster than they can go. Some fruit ripens faster than others. People are not all the same, neither do they all respond at the same rate of speed. Some are slower, some faster. The Scripture says: "And he said, So is the kingdom of God, as if a man should cast seed into the ground; and should sleep, and rise night and day, and the seed should spring and grow up, he knoweth not how. For the earth bringeth forth fruit of herself; first the blade, then the ear, after that the full corn in the ear. But when the fruit is brought forth, immediately he putteth in the sickle, because the harvest is come" (Mark 4:26-29). Pull only when you feel fairly certain the fish is well hooked; pluck only when you believe the fruit is ripe for harvest.

9. Don't talk with a person about joining the church in the presence of their friends. Never attempt to gain a decision in the presence of those who have not been under the same influence. Peer pressure is usually detrimental to the decision-making process. Sometimes the candidate is not spiritually mature or strong enough to make a public confession. If pressured to make a decision under public circumstances, he or she may reject the appeal. This may permanently close the door to that person.

10. Never overurge or give the sense that you are pressuring. Sometimes a person may be suffering from "truth saturation." Because of this, the individual may give the impression that he or she is pulling away, demonstrating a very normal response to pressure. But at this point, a relief from pressure may be the candidate's greatest need. Pray earnestly that the Spirit Himself will add the gentle urging needed.

11. Don't give the impression that you are in a hurry, even if you are. This is in reference to your visit to secure a decision. You never want the candidate to feel that he or she must hurry up and make a choice. On the contrary, when you are working toward a decision, you should give the candidate all the time necessary to comfortably choose a course of action.

12. Avoid staying for refreshments after the decision is secured. Once a person has been led to make a decision, you want to allow the atmosphere you've just created to remain in the home for as long as possible. Though the candidate may offer you something, tell the individual that you just want him or her to spend time with the Lord, reflecting on his or her decision.

Factors Affecting Spiritual Decisions

There are many factors that hinder individuals from making effective decisions besides their ignorance concerning the methods of the Holy Spirit. These factors revolve around their own individual fears, their seemingly unsolvable challenges and insurmountable obstacles, which the devil brings their way. It must be remembered that this is a new track for individuals who are just waking up spiritually; this is a path that they have not trodden upon. They need time to develop enough faith to begin the trek toward heaven. Therefore, all the encouragement that can be given, all help available to alleviate arising problems should be made available.

The following is a list of the different social, economic, and spiritual factors that often serve as hindrances to individuals who desire to make a decision for Christ, or who need to be encouraged toward that step.

Economic Factors

This important factor, when used as the basis of an objection, may assume several forms. Here are some of them.

"I would follow your teachings, but it would cost me my job." Suggestion: Assure the person sympathetically that you understand and, above all, that God understands. From Matthew 6:25-33 you can share with him or her God's advice under such circumstances. Faith-building testimonies, personal experiences, and scripture can be used profitably at this point.

"My husband has threatened to withdraw his support if I unite with you." Suggestion: Avoid saying anything critical about her husband. Rather, *tactfully* remind her that

her allegiance is to God first. Psalm 27:10 and Matthew 10:37-39 are good texts to use at this point. She should be told that her obedience would help her husband's understanding, since his opposition undoubtedly springs from misunderstanding.

"I cannot afford to keep the Sabbath. If I do, I may lose my job, and I have a lot of debt." Suggestion: Remind the candidate that God is the giver of all good gifts—all the possessions he or she already has, God has provided. Such texts as Deuteronomy 8:18; 28:3-6; and Matthew 16:26 are useful at this point. Share with the person scriptures of encouragement, such as Psalm 37:25, as well as the experiences of others.

"If I have to pay tithe in order to join your church, I don't believe I would make it financially." Suggestion: Have the individual read Malachi 3:6-8. Emphasize that if one is faithful to God, the Master will not let him or her down. He will multiply what remains. The *grateful* will be *faithful* in their giving. Again, stories of other people's experiences in this matter are very helpful. However, the most powerful testimony is that of your own.

Social Factors

Opposition of friends. Suggestion: Luke 6:22, 23; Proverbs 18:24. Help the candidates understand that, unfortunately, this happens all too often. Mark 3:21 shows how Jesus' friends thought He was crazy. Lead them to see that the friendship of Christ is to be prized above all else.

Opposition within the home. Suggestion: Matthew 19:29. Focus on the promise given. One must be very cautious; handle this objection with tact and care. Matthew 10:34-37 clearly states the issues involved. However, always remember that "blood is thicker than water" and that this concept should lead the worker to exercise utmost care in this matter.

"*I don't believe I need to attend church. I can worship God at home.*" Suggestion: 1 John 2:15. This may give evidence that the person is not yet sufficiently convicted on this issue. Read what God asks of him or her in Hebrews 10:25 and Leviticus 23:1, 3. Assure the person that he or she will find pleasure and support in fellowship with the people of God. Help the individual understand that to follow Jesus fully is to follow His example, and He attended church. (See Luke 4:16.)

Spiritual Factors Affecting Decisions

"*I don't think it is right to leave the church of my childhood.*" Suggestion: Acts 2:37-41 and Revelation 18:4. Cite the example of Jesus, who after 30 years left His home (Matthew 24:1 and 16:18). Encourage the individual to follow Jesus, rather than any church (Matthew 7:21, 22).

"*I am not sure that I could continue even if I begin. It would be a shame to backslide.*" Suggestion: Help candidates to understand that we generally do not think this way in other areas. Just think of the things that we begin every day, not knowing if we can finish them. We apply for a job, not knowing if we are going to continue in it. When a couple marries, are they certain that they will be together 10 years hence? The answer obviously is no. But they have two elements acting on their side—faith and love. That is enough to begin with. Share texts such as Philippians 1:6; Romans 8:37-39; Jude 24; 1 Peter 1:7.

"*I plan to join, but I wish to practice for a few weeks before joining to be sure that I can live it.*" Suggestion: Mark 4:19, 20 and Luke 9:59-62. You cannot live it. Christ must live it in you. Point them to Galatians 2:20. Your chances are best in the church, where you have the encouragement of fellow believers and Spirit-filled messages from the pulpit to strengthen and support you.

"I can't seem to make a decision, although I know the teachings are of God." Suggestion: Help the person understand how the Holy Spirit works and how important it is to yield to His convicting power (John 14:16, 26; 16:7-11). The problem lies in one's inability to surrender. Help the candidate see that there is a battle being fought for the ownership of his or her soul, and that the only safety is in surrendering to the Lord (1 Peter 5:8; Luke 22:31, 32).

"Can't I live what you teach in my church?" Suggestion: It is difficult to swim against the current. The odds would definitely be against your ability to maintain your new beliefs. How can you follow the teachings of Jesus in a place where His teachings are not being followed? In an institution that teaches another faith, the pressure will always pull you in the wrong direction. This is the reason for the warnings recorded in 2 Corinthians 6:14-17 and Revelation 18:4. You cannot try to follow a dual religious experience and succeed in spirituality.

"My past life condemns me. I am discouraged because I have been such a great sinner." Suggestion: Have candidates read 1 John 1:9 and John 8:11. Lead them to accept the reality that forgiveness and salvation were the sole purpose for Jesus' coming. He came to deliver us from the power of sin, cleansing us from our past sins. Read also Romans 6:3-7, 1 Timothy 1:15-17, and Romans 3:23. The Bible contains many precious promises that give us great encouragement. Isaiah 44:22, Proverbs 28:13, and many others assure us that God will blot out our sinful past as we consecrate our lives to Him for the future.

Chapter 13

Clearing the Candidate

The object of all the foregoing is to help the person make a complete decision to accept Christ and become a disciple. Baptism should then logically follow just as a love relationship finally blossoms into a wedding celebration. Scripture says, "For by one Spirit are we all baptized into one body" (1 Corinthians 12:13). And in Ephesians 1:22, 23 we read, "And hath put all *things* under his feet, and gave him *to be* the head over all *things* to the church, which is his body, the fulness of him that filleth all in all." So a person accepts Jesus and His truth, and then is baptized into His body, which is the church.

There is a natural question that arises. What are the steps that contribute to this happy marriage? And what's necessary to bring a person to this point? Let us consider several things essential to arrive at this junction. It is imperative to understand that all of the elements mentioned in the previous chapters must be in place. In other words, there must be Spirit-filled truth given to the candidate. Conviction should be present in the candidate, evident by those indicators already discussed. Just as a fruit tree bears fruit, so must there be obvious fruit in the life of the one experiencing the promptings of the Holy Spirit.

A prerequisite to baptism is leading a person to accept Christ as a personal Saviour. This has already been covered in a previous chapter. If this has not been done already, a person should be led (or has been led by conviction) to sense his or her need of accepting Christ as a personal Saviour. Once that felt need is realized, the instructor should walk the individual through the process of accepting Christ. As the person continues studying and growing in understanding (whether in a public evangelistic setting or in a series of Bible studies) the time will come when an evangelistic sermon or Bible study needs to be given, outlining the concept of baptism and its meaning and requirement. Texts normally used are: Romans 6:1-6, John 3:1-3, etc.

At the appropriate time an appeal should be made to candidates to accept the rite of baptism. This should be encouraged as a public confession of their inward experience of a relationship to the Saviour, and their desire and willingness to be washed of their sins, and to follow Him all the way in the Christian life. If in response to an appeal (whether in public or private) they yield to the invitation and make a public or private decision, then they need to be cleared for baptism.

The Clearing

Now comes the time to prepare the candidate for baptism. This process is called clearing in evangelistic circles. At this time there should be in the instructor's possession a clearing card. This card contains the general tenets of the Adventist cardinal points of faith. These general points are often placed in the back of a baptismal certificate, or can be found in the Seventh-day Adventist *Church Manual* or printed on a small pocket-sized card. At times these can be found printed in the back of some churches' bulletins. An effort should be made to secure a clearing list preparatory to making a visit with the interest. And please remember!

Leading a person to be readied for baptism can be done by a layperson. In other words, it does not *have* to be done by a pastor.

Let's consider the steps needed to be taken to walk the candidate through the process. Let us suppose the individual has responded to a public appeal for baptism and either annotates that desire on a decision card or demonstrates it by standing or the raising of hands. Once the decision is made, always seal the decision with prayer. For example, if the decision is made in the home, then pray with the person, acknowledging the fact that he or she made that choice with God's help. If the persons have responded to a public call, then offer a prayer in which you thank God that they yielded to His wonderful Spirit.

The next step is to meet with that person. The instructor should go prepared for the task. There should be a Bible, a decision card, and prior personal heart preparation. Upon arriving, let him or her know early on your intention and purpose. In other words, after the usual greeting, the instructor should say, "John, I am so excited about your decision to follow your Lord." (Always affirm the fact that the decision made was between them and the Lord. This is very important.) "I have come to help you prepare for that wonderful moment." Find a place where (if you are not already there) you can spend the time with the candidate in privacy and quietness. (Caution should be taken with the opposite sex—always be where you can be visible if you are alone. However, it is always well to have someone along with you whom the candidate knows and is comfortable with.) Then, facing the candidate, say: "On the decision card that you turned in last night [or whenever it was—two days ago, etc.], you checked the box requesting baptism. This is wonderful! Have you ever been baptized by immersion before?" Wait for the response.

If the answer is no, then proceed with the following. "One of the most wonderful biblical ordinances ordained of God is baptism. As you recall, it represents the death, burial, and resurrection of Jesus. It also symbolizes the washing away of all our sins. Isn't that wonderful?" Wait for the response. "In order to help you get prepared, I would like to review some of the basic tenets of the Christian faith. I would also like to explain how the ceremony is done so you can participate in it with peace and confidence.

"In my hand I have a list of points to review. But first, let us pray." Then bow your head and pray. When you pray, make mention of the joy over John's decision, give thanks for God's mercy in speaking to his heart, and ask God's blessing as you spend time together. This prayer should be short and to the point.

Now with the card in hand, begin by asking the candidate the questions on the card. Emphasize that what you want to do is see what he or she is clear on. An individual going over a list of 14 points and discovering he or she has problems with only two of them will be encouraged to see that he or she is pretty close. If something is not clear, and is not a major issue, address it. If it is a major issue, then place a check by the question and tell the candidate that you will cover it later in greater detail. Cover only four points at a sitting. On the first points of faith most Christians or non-Christians usually have no problems if they have been studying a series of studies or have been attending an evangelistic meeting.

After you finish with the first four points, ask this question: "John, we have covered these four points. How do you feel about them; are you clear?" Wait for the answer. Most of the time John will feel relieved that the points were basic in nature. Affirm the fact that he is doing well, and then have a closing prayer. Again, in this prayer thanks should be offered for the steps John is taking, ask God to continue to lead him as he continues to prepare himself for the baptismal service.

The next time you get together, refresh John's commitment in your prayer. Then proceed with the card. Again, go over four points or five. This, of course, depends on the candidate and how much exposure he or she has had prior to this preparation process. In some cases this review can be done much faster if the candidate has already had Bible studies and has demonstrated acceptance of the teachings. In other cases, such as in an evangelistic meeting, it may go a little slower. This again is determined by the foreknowledge the individual has concerning the points of faith.

Once the complete list has been covered, then the following question should be asked: "John, which date would you prefer?" At this juncture he should not be asked if he now wants to be baptized. This should already be a foregone conclusion. You should already have an idea when the next baptismal date or dates are scheduled for. Or the pastor who would be officiating should be asked when it would be a good time. Then with this knowledge, present the candidate with a choice of dates.

It is now time to give the card to the candidate and have him or her fill out the back of it. There should be a place for their legal name, address, date of birth, and the chosen date of baptism. Once the card is filled out, ask to take the card into your possession, explaining to the candidate that this information will be used to make the baptismal certificate. You should now give him or her a copy of the baptismal vows for the keeping.

At this point, explain the details of the ceremony. Give

the candidate an example of how the baptism is to be performed. If possible, demonstrate with the candidate so as to enable him or her to feel comfortable with what will happen. After this, inform the candidate that all he or she needs to bring is a change of undergarments (that is, if the church is providing the baptismal gowns and towels). Ask the candidate to bring a change of clothing if this is warranted. Sometimes he or she will need to bring a handkerchief or washcloth if the church is not providing these. Be explicit concerning the time and location of the ceremony. And if it is necessary, provide a map with instructions. On occasions it may be helpful to offer the person transportation to facilitate his or her arriving on time. All of this contributes to alleviating any anxiety concerning the unknown and allaying any fears the candidate may have about the ceremony.

It is always advisable to keep the officiating minister appraised about the candidate's progress and decision. At times the pastor may want to have a brief review with the candidate. If that is the pastor's desire, this is appropriate— for the officiating minister is the one who will have to be clear that the candidate is truly ready for this step.

Removing the Objections

The enemy always storms individuals who are under the convicting power of God. Consequently, the devil will raise objections and problems to serve as obstacles to the sincere seeker. Because of this phenomenon the instructor must be on alert to help. So let me cover this concern with the following example.

A spouse of the potential candidate approached me, asking if I could visit her nonmember husband. I consented and made an appointment to see him. When I arrived I did the usual get-acquainted steps. The best way to get acquainted is to spend the time asking questions that people like to answer. These questions are concerning the job, the family, and mutual hobbies that may bond you to the person and perhaps his or her upbringing. For example you may ask, "Did you grow up in this city?" etc. Then at the appropriate moment this conversation needs to shift to the spiritual. This process I call *diagnostic questioning*. Just as the doctor tries to ascertain what the problem is by asking questions, so must we when trying to get to the bottom of the spiritual ailment.

So I asked, "Sy, how long have you been attending the church?" (The wife had informed me that he attended church on a regular basis.)

He replied, "For about 10 years."

"You've been attending for a good while, I see. You must like that church," I responded.

"Yes, I do" was his answer. This let me know that he was positive with the church and its practices.

"When did you become a member?" I asked. (I knew he was not a member, but it is important for me not to assume anything. It is also important to use these lead-in questions to see how the person is thinking.)

He said, "I am not a member."

"Is there anything that would keep you from becoming a member?" I asked.

At this point it is important to listen to the objection. I waited and then he responded. He retorted with "I can't believe that my mother was worshiping the devil!"

What an objection! Frankly, his objection did not mean anything to me. So I had to ask to get a better handle on this. "What do you mean?" I questioned.

Here is where he opened up. He then asked me,

"Don't you people teach that the beast of Revelation is the Catholic Church? And that the devil is the one who is behind it, right?"

"Yes," I answered hesitantly.

"If I accept that, then I have to accept that my mother was praying to the devil, and I can't do that. She was a godly woman," he said.

What a revelation! Here was the objection. Now my task was to remove the objection so that I could return to the first key question.

"Say, what did she pray about?" I quizzed.

"She prayed about a lot of things, especially for me," he replied.

When he said this, I noticed tears welling up in his eyes. "Was she concerned about you?" I asked.

"Yes," he replied. "I was an alcoholic, and this caused my mother great grief."

"Are you still an alcoholic?"

"No!" he triumphantly responded.

"Well," I asked, "who answered that prayer?"

He looked at me with a troubled look and then said, "God did." I then proceeded to explain to him that his mother's prayers were answered by the One she had been praying to. I also let him know that I believed that if his mother were alive, she would be rejoicing and thanking God for that answered prayer.

The objection being met, then I had to return to the key question. "Is there anything that would keep you from joining the church?" To this he told me he had a Sabbath work problem. I affirmed that the God who answered his mother's prayer could resolve that problem. We prayed together, and I left. He went to his employers and asked for the Sabbath off. After two weeks God did answer the prayer, and Sy's obstacle was removed. Once again I went to the key question.

"Is there anything that will keep you now?"

"No!" he replied. In a few weeks preparations were made, and Sy was baptized.

Please remember to be in continued and earnest prayer. Oftentimes the enemy will do all he can to keep the person from following through with their decision. In the event that a challenge arises, it is expedient that the instructor do all in their power to help the candidate overcome the challenge. Always do what you can to remove the obstacle, and then return to the key question: *Is there anything that will keep you from . . . ?* Once the person sees his or her way clear, it is just a matter of time till there will be joy in heaven over one sinner who repents. And the greatest reward will be experienced by the one who labored to bring one to Christ.

Chapter 14

Texts on Decisions

The following list is provided to aid the soul winner with texts that can be utilized in helping candidates in their decisions. It may be well to make a copy and place it in their Bible.

The need for immediate decision:
Psalm 18:44; 119:60
Matthew 4:19, 20
Acts 22:16
Hebrews 4:7

The danger of putting the decision off:
Matthew 19:16-22
Matthew 13:45, 46
Luke 14:33
John 12:35
2 Corinthians 6:2
2 Corinthians 8:9

How to receive Christ as one's personal Saviour:
John 3:16
John 1:12, 13
Galatians 2:20
Revelation 3:20

How to find forgiveness:
  Psalm 32:5
  Proverbs 28:13
  Isaiah 1:18
  1 John 1:9

The keeping power of Christ:
  Psalm 37:23, 24
  Philippians 1:6
  Hebrews 7:25
  Jude 24

How to find victory:
  2 Chronicles 32:7, 8
  John 1:12
  1 Corinthians 15:57
  Philippians 4:13
  1 John 5:4

Assurance of acceptance:
  Isaiah 1:19, 20
  John 5:24
  John 6:37
  2 Corinthians 8:12

Increased light to come:
  Proverbs 4:18
  Daniel 12:4
  John 12:35, 36

Encouragement to keep the Sabbath:
  Isaiah 56:1-6; 58:13, 14
  Ezekiel 20:20

Revelation 22:14

MEETING EXCUSES WITH SCRIPTURE

"I can't leave my church."
John 12:26, 27, 42, 43
Revelation 18:4
Matthew 7:22, 23

"I can't make a living if I keep the Sabbath."
Matthew 6:33
Psalm 37:3
Isaiah 65:13, 14
Psalm 37:25

"I will lose my job if I keep the Sabbath."
Matthew 16:25, 26
1 Timothy 4:8

"It is inconvenient to follow the doctrine of Sabbathkeeping."
Matthew 16:24; 10:38
Hebrews 7:25
Isaiah 1:18

"I am too great a sinner."
1 Timothy 1:15

"I am afraid I can't hold out."
Jude 24

"I can't live up to the truth."
1 Corinthians 10:13

2 Corinthians 8:12
John 1:12

"I am not good enough."

2 Corinthians 8:12

"People will talk about me."

John 17:14
Luke 6:22, 23, 26
Proverbs 29:25

"My friends will ridicule me."

John 15:19
Mark 8:34
James 4:4

"My husband [wife, father, mother, brother, sister, etc.] will oppose me."

Matthew 10:36, 37
Luke 14:26, 27

"My preacher and my friends advise me against this."

1 Kings 13:1–26
Acts 4:19; 5:29

"It will cause division in my home if I stand for this teaching."

Luke 12:49-53
1 Kings 18:17, 18

"There is one thing [jewelry, tobacco, etc.] I

cannot give up."
Matthew 19:16-22; 6:24
Luke 14:33
Matthew 13:45, 46
1 Corinthians 8:13

"No, not now."
Proverbs 27:1
2 Corinthians 6:2
Hebrews 3:13
Genesis 6:3
Isaiah 55:6

"I'll wait for my husband [wife, friend, etc.] so we can accept it together."
Ezekiel 14:20
Ezekiel 18:20
Romans 14:2

"I will wait until I have the right kind of feeling."
Isaiah 48:18
1 John 2:3

Remember, not all will surrender and turn their lives over to the Lord. Our Saviour Himself suffered grief because of those who, though they were called, still chose to turn away (John 6:66). Nevertheless, this did not keep Him from continuing His efforts to reach those who might eventually respond and accept Him as Lord of their lives. But the joy that comes when one soul turns to the Lord is summed up in the statement "I say unto you, that likewise joy shall be in heaven over one sinner that repenteth, more than over ninety and nine just persons, which need no repentance" (Luke 15:7). And again He says, "Likewise, I say unto you, there is joy in the presence of the angels of God over one sinner that repenteth" (verse 10).

I would like to leave you with these words spoken by Mrs. Ellen G. White at the close of one of her meetings: "The end of all things is at hand. Are we ready to meet Christ when He shall appear? Will He say to us, 'Come, ye blessed of My Father; enter into the city'? When we see the great reward that is in store for the faithful, how our hearts should reach out after others, that they might receive the light. You know not how many hearts are really thirsting for the waters of life, but here is the Bible to open before them. Will you do it? Will you act like men and women that expect the Lord to come? Will you have living faith, and pray as never before? Will you wrestle with God as Jacob wrestled with Him—'I will not let thee go, except thou bless me'? And when His blessing rests upon you, you will be anxious to have others receive it."*

---

* Ellen G. White, *Manuscript Releases,* vol. 19, p. 139.